ASPIRE: 100 PROJECTS
TO STRENGTHEN YOUR
ACTING SKILLS

ASPIRE: 100 PROJECTS
TO STRENGTHEN YOUR
ACTING SKILLS

Jona Howl

All inquiries should be addressed to:
Barron's Educational Series, Inc.
250 Wireless Boulevard
Hauppauge, NY 11788
www.barronseduc.com

ISBN-13: 978-0-7641-3949-9
ISBN-10: 0-7641-3949-5

Library of Congress Control Number: 2008927162

QUAR.GYDC

Conceived, designed, and produced by
Quarto Publishing plc
The Old Brewery
6 Blundell Street
London N7 9BH

Project editor: **Trisha Telep**
Designer: **James Lawrence**
Art director: **Caroline Guest**
Picture researcher: **Sarah Bell**
Photographer: **Deborah Rowe**
Illustrator: **Dermot Gallagher**
Copy editor: **Bryan Doubt**
Proofreader: **Sue Edwards**
Indexer: **Diana Le Core**
Additional text: **Dee Cannon**

Creative director: **Moira Clinch**
Publisher: **Paul Carslake**

Color separation by Sang Choy International
Pte Ltd., Singapore
Printed by Star Standard Industries (PTE) Limited,
Singapore

9 8 7 6 5 4 3 2 1

Contents

Chapter 1: Posture   Chapter 2: Movement

Chapter 3: Voice 38

Chapter 4: Performing Text 58

Chapter 5: Character 74

Chapter 6: The Audition 94

Chapter 3: Voice   Chapter 4: Performing Text   Chapter 5: Character   Chapter 6: The Audition

Introduction

Theater school auditions are a minefield. The best schools take only a small number of students each year, which means your dream of becoming an actor can easily crumble if you're not well prepared. There are many people with a great deal of talent out there, so why is it that they don't necessarily get in?

There are a number of reasons, mostly based on the fact that theater schools have very set ideas about what constitutes "good acting" and how to teach it. Therefore they tend to accept students who they think will most fit into the training systems they already have in place. Some schools prefer you to be a little older with more worldly experience, while others prefer applicants with no experience whatsoever. Similarly, some schools like you to be emotionally open and volatile, while others may be looking for a more intellectual, considered approach.

All theater schools, however, search for one basic element above all others: potential. This is usually judged by assessing the applicant's natural spontaneity and basic sense of "aliveness." Aspiring actors need to move and speak as openly and honestly as possible with absolute freedom and total synchronicity.

Many professional actors put their success down to understanding the practical side of the entertainment industry. Put quite simply: They find out what to do and how to do it. And you need to do the same. You have to develop a detailed plan with clear goals and then set about methodically achieving them. This is not a fail-proof guarantee for success but it will certainly increase your chances.

This book represents your plan of attack. It is a step-by-step guide—a coaching program—that will get you into better audition shape. Designed to energize you, educate your movement, and liberate your voice, it will also help you choose and perform audition pieces. There are even tips on what to wear on the day itself, leaving as little as possible to chance.

Some people will tell you that acting can't be taught. Most teachers disagree. This includes one of the masters, Konstantin Stanislavski, who introduced a method of teaching still used in many theater schools today. Indeed, the fact that there are theater schools at all tells you that acting is an art form that can be studied, learned, and improved on.

It's good to dream but often dreaming is not enough.
Let's get to work.

Acting is a craft

Good acting is a well-honed craft. But if a craftsperson has to work with blunt tools, then no matter how gifted the craftsperson is, their results will not be refined. With sharp tools, hard work produces exciting results. As an actor, *you* are the tool of your trade. You have to get *yourself* into sharp "acting" shape to achieve the results you desire. Concentrate on these three main areas to impress at an audition:

Vibrancy

Consider this scenario. You are a theater-school director in a room full of good actors, all of them showing equal potential. Who would you choose and why? The chances are that you would be naturally attracted to individuals with the most vitality; those who were genuinely bright and energized. As an actor, high levels of uninhibited, focused, natural energy will always get you noticed.

Theatrical awareness

You also need to know how to energize the space in which you work. This is a process in which you channel your heightened energy levels to affect the audience around you. Theatrical awareness also includes the practical rules of stagecraft (for example, information about where to stand on the stage and why).

Control

Finally, you need to show the kind of determination, self-discipline, and emotional strength that will allow you to work toward a goal and not crack under the intense pressure of theater school. The panel want to see that you have what it takes to stay the course and continue to work as a professional after your training has been completed.

Patience is a virtue

You must develop patience if you are serious about becoming an actor:

- *TV and film work is at least 90% sitting around, waiting for your shot.*
- *Film makeup can take from two to six hours every day.*
- *During a technical rehearsal of a play you may be waiting days before actually setting foot on the stage.*
- *Getting the "call back" could take days, weeks, or even months as projects stall, casting requirements change, and budgets are revised.*

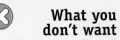 **What you want**
To have naturally flowing energy.

What you don't want
To be pretending to be energized or to be working on pure nervous energy.

This is counterproductive to your craft and may get you noticed by the panel in a less than positive way.

About this book

This book is organized into six main chapters focusing on building aspects of the actor's repertoire; the sixth chapter tells you how to apply for and win an audition. The content is structured around workouts—practical exercises that you can do at home, mostly on your own, sometimes with a friend. Each workout is tailored to sharpen your acting skills, and make you better prepared to shine at an audition. At the end of the book (pages 120–126) are recommendations for audition pieces for men and women.

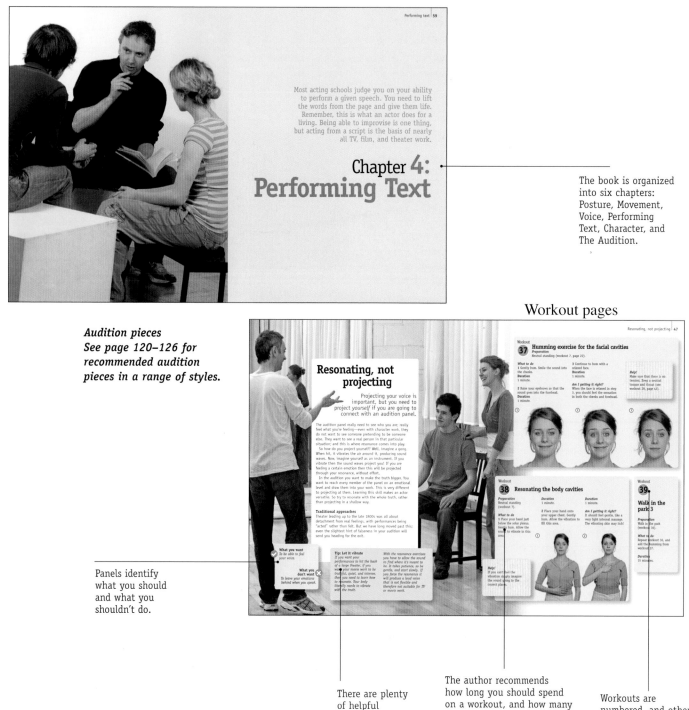

Most acting schools judge you on your ability to perform a given speech. You need to lift the words from the page and give them life. Remember, this is what an actor does for a living. Being able to improvise is one thing, but acting from a script is the basis of nearly all TV, film, and theater work.

Chapter 4:
Performing Text

The book is organized into six chapters: Posture, Movement, Voice, Performing Text, Character, and The Audition.

Audition pieces
See page 120–126 for recommended audition pieces in a range of styles.

Workout pages

Panels identify what you should and what you shouldn't do.

There are plenty of helpful coaching tips.

The author recommends how long you should spend on a workout, and how many times an exercise should be repeated.

Workouts are numbered, and other workouts cross-refer back to them.

Using the workouts and programs

Start by skimming through the entire book to get a sense of what is involved. Then tackle each chapter and work through them at the rate of roughly one chapter per week. Try each and every workout in the book, and then, at the end of the chapter, try the designated program you find there.

Some of the workouts might feel boring and repetitious, with only subtle changes between them, but these are the basics that are going to change your acting life.

Every actor's foundation is built through repetition of good, basic practice. Acting is not always exciting. For a true actor, however, the excitement comes from that basic, journeyman-like work. These are the basic activities that need to be constantly reinforced if you are going to pursue acting as a profession.

At the end of each chapter, you'll find a weekly program to follow.

Follow this sequence of workouts for one week.

The mini-programs are bite-sized and quick to do.

More advanced?

If after reading the book you realize that some topics are very familiar and cover old ground, begin by practicing the sections you really need. But remember that all aspects of acting are interrelated so, once you have sorted out any areas of weakness, it's a good idea to jump to the final program and to use this for your daily exercise.

But I don't have much time!
Those who don't have much time can follow the mini-programs which contain a selection of the most important exercises from that chapter. Also, if you need to speed up the training, study the chapters in reverse. It goes without saying, however, that you will get much better results if you work through each chapter completely.

1 Eat the right food

Most research says that to increase vitality you have to eat plenty of food that is great for your body. Remember to eat well: have lots of fresh vegetables and whole grains with your meals, and drink plenty of water. Cut down on dairy and fatty foods and decrease your caffeine and sugar intake.

Top tip from the professionals—keep hydrated—great for body, mind, and skin!

2 Be reliable but not predictable

Don't lose your edge by following the crowd. Surround yourself with energetic individuals and hang out with people who have similar goals to your own and a positive sense of direction.

Yoga is great for strengthening body and mind.

10 easy ways to increase your levels of

6 Get the balance right

Take time to step outside of yourself and to check that work and play are balanced. It is essential to work hard but also important to have a release from that work, and return to it later with renewed energy. And, whatever you do, always maintain a sense of humor about yourself.

7 Act

Get involved in as much to do with acting as you can, regardless of level, project, or whether you are acting yourself or coaching others. All experience is valuable.

8 Attend live stage performances

Go to the theater on a regular basis and keep abreast of yearly fall and spring programs. Aim to see as much as possible, good and bad, amateur and professional. The content and execution of a top-level production will be relevant to your preparation; likewise, poor productions can help to pinpoint your problem areas. When you go to the movies, carefully observe the performances of the actors on screen.

Study other forms of creativity: go to galleries, music concerts, and the ballet, where creative input and dramatic delivery are still key.

3 Take regular exercise

Remember that you're strengthening, toning, and building. The aim is to become physically fit and mentally alert, not to exercise to total exhaustion. Get good at one particular form of exercise as this will give you a depth of fitness and confidence. Make sure you do other forms as well, in order to keep it varied.

4 Don't hide behind an "image"

Avoid going for a certain look just because you think it might help "show off" your personality. Allow your personality to shine through without resorting to gimmicks. Wear clothes that suit you, not clothes that define you.

5 Spend time outdoors

Going for regular walks in natural settings is extremely beneficial. Not only does it clear your head and allow you to put things into perspective but it also encourages a sense of liberation. After a bout of brisk walking, sit still on a park bench. See how you feel.

vibrancy, theatrical awareness, and control

9 Get some sleep

This really helps revitalize physical and mental energy levels. The most basic of routines works wonders.

10 Be committed to success

If learning to act is more important than anything else, then make finding time to learn the most important thing you do. Make a general plan and stick to it. If it doesn't work then make another one. Keep going until you arrive where you want to be.

Start keeping a journal and a detailed plan of action.

Build your own fitness program

Work this fitness routine around your life on a daily, weekly, and monthly basis. Adhere to it without interruptions for the period of time that you study this book. This program may seem a little like a military regime at first, but it's nothing of the sort. It's about gradually building the healthy eating habits and exercise choices that will fine-tune you for the task of being an actor. Your health and fitness is the basis around which the imaginative and creative skills are developed.

Week 1
DAILY

Monday to Friday
- Eat plenty of healthy food for breakfast and lunch. Eat what you want for dinner.
- Exercise.
- Get plenty of sleep.
- Drink lots of water.

Saturday & Sunday
- Eat plenty of healthy food for breakfast. Eat what you like for lunch and dinner.
- Drink lots of water.
- Go out with friends.
- No exercising allowed.

This week
- Who needs money? Find some free theater happening around town. Watch street performers, children's theater, charity events. See as much live performance as you possibly can.

Week 2
DAILY

Monday, Wednesday, & Friday
- Eat plenty of healthy food for breakfast, lunch, and dinner.
- Exercise.
- Get plenty of sleep.
- Drink lots of water.

Tuesday & Thursday
- Eat plenty of healthy food for breakfast and lunch. Eat what you want for dinner.
- Exercise every day.
- Get plenty of sleep.
- Drink lots of water.

Saturday & Sunday
- Eat plenty of healthy food for breakfast and lunch. Eat whatever you like for dinner.
- Drink lots of water.
- Go to a free creative place.
- Go out with friends.

This week
- Book tickets to see a professional play.

Weeks 3 and 4
DAILY

Monday to Friday
- Eat plenty of healthy food for breakfast, lunch, and dinner.
- Exercise.
- Get plenty of sleep.
- Drink lots of water.

Saturday & Sunday
- Eat plenty of healthy food for two meals out of three (your choice).
- Exercise one day; rest one day.
- Drink lots of water.
- Go to an art gallery.
- Have a night out with friends.

This week
- Volunteer to help at your local elementary school's annual play.

What now?
By the end of the month your routine will be in place. This is the one you stick to. If you really need to change things around now then plan the changes in advance. Don't be spontaneous. Be strong.

This program is about taking control. If you mess up, then re-group and start again. Keep your eyes on the prize. Ask yourself constantly: "Why am I doing this?" It might be a motivating idea to make a wall chart and tick off your successes day by day.

Do one thing now. Straight away. Make a list, eat something good for your body, or go for a run.

Put the book down now and do it!

Tip: Have a check-up

If you're in any doubt about your health, or have any physical issues, make sure that you get yourself checked out by a professional before you change your diet or before attempting any of the exercises included in this book.

The **Course**

If you want your body to respond well to your instincts as an actor, good alignment will guarantee a natural flow of energy through your body. Tuning your physical instrument in this way creates a sensation of effortlessness and freedom, with all parts moving together harmoniously.

Chapter **1: Posture**

The Alexander Technique

Several years ago, good posture meant a pole-straight back and artificially stiff, overly controlled movement. These days, good alignment is all about creating a strong, balanced, and flexible spine. One effective approach often used by actors is the Alexander Technique. On these pages you'll learn a few basic exercises inspired by the Alexander Technique, and fused with other exercise methods, like Pilates.

History

As a young actor, Frederick Alexander (1869–1955) developed chronic laryngitis. When physical tension was at its height, his voice and general stage presence would falter. Doctors failed to help him, so he set about developing his own cure based on observing himself in the mirror as he spoke. He noticed that a slight change in the position of the head involved a significant reduction in any unnecessary neck and throat tension. Realizing he held additional tension in other parts of his back, he began to move down the spine and the Alexander Technique was born.

Applications

The original technique has since evolved and we'll be looking at a mixture of traditional and modern approaches. The process is about gradually building up strength and flexibility. By carefully examining how human beings perform ordinary actions, such as sitting, walking, running, standing, lifting, and speaking, Alexander speculated that anyone could be "taught" to identify unnecessary tension in their movements and reduce it without forcing or straining.

Note that these exercises are only *inspired* by the Alexander Technique. You need to seek out a qualified teacher if you actually wish to study this truly revolutionary technique.

Workout

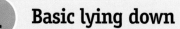

1 **Basic lying down**

Preparation
Collect books of varying thicknesses and stack them on the floor in front of you. Stand naturally against a wall (make sure that your back and shoulder blades touch the wall). Focus on a spot in front of you at eye level.

Notice the gap between the back of your head and the wall.

Have a friend use the books to fill the gap between your head and the wall. The books that fill the gap now become your "pillow" for the exercise to come.

Be careful not to overfill or underfill the gap.

Basic lying down position
Lie down on the floor. Place your "pillow" from the preparation (see above) under your head.

Face and shoulders relaxed.

Hands resting on stomach.

Feet and knees parallel.

What you want
To feel the whole of the back area (including the shoulders) relaxing, totally supported by the firmness of the floor.

What you don't want
The feeling that your back is sinking into the floor. For maximum effect it must be relaxing onto a solid floor with the feeling that it is being absolutely held and supported.

You shouldn't feel compression in the front of your throat.

Correct neck position.

Help!
My legs shake.
• This is perfectly normal at the start. The trembling is the intermediate stage of this process. If your body has been out of alignment for a while, repositioning it correctly may take time.

Place the heels close to the body.

Feet too far away.

Tip: Hello yawn!
Welcome any yawns at the end of the exercise to open up the mouth and throat.

Duration
Lie down for 15 minutes (use a timer) allow yourself to feel relaxed and powerful. When you have finished stretch out slowly and carefully.

Workout

2 **Intermediate lying down**

The actor's focus is on his stomach muscles.

The pelvic tilt is very subtle. Can you spot it?

What you want
It should feel freeing and relaxing.

What you don't want
To tense the neck, shoulders, or upper chest.

Preparation
Basic lying down (workout 1) (10 minutes).

What to do
Move your hands from your hips and place them out to your sides, palms down. Now imagine the spine lengthening.

Keeping the chest, shoulders, neck, and pelvis area relaxed, contract the muscles at the sides of the waist inward toward the spine. At the same time pull the stomach muscles downward toward the spine.

Tip: Engage
When relaxing after the exercise become aware of your breathing. It is through the awareness of the breath that your mind becomes actively engaged.

Holding that contraction, breathe in by expanding the lower ribs. Now contract the stomach muscles still further so that the hips gently tilt toward you. Hold and relax.

Duration
Repeat 10 times.

After-exercise relaxation
This is the basic after-exercise relaxation for many of the exercises. It is beneficial for you to get familiar with this basic position.
Once you have finished the exercise, stretch out slowly and carefully. Allow the hips to open. Totally relax for one or two minutes. Get up slowly. Now sit down for a minute or two. Don't think about anything. Just "be."

Strength and balance

Now you've mastered the basic position, it's time to add another exercise to increase your flexibility and core strength. This will add consistency to your positioning.

Workout

Advanced lying down

Preparation
Basic lying down (workout 1), for 5 minutes.
Intermediate lying down (workout 2), 5 repetitions.

What to do
Instead of relaxing, keep rolling your hips toward you until you find yourself in position **a** (photo, right).

Easy does it. No straining.

Now raise your hands over your head to the floor (position **b**). Remain like this for a count of 10. Slowly roll the spine back down to the floor.

Now gently tilt the hips very slightly away from you. Tilt back to neutral. Remain in this position (with arms stretched above your head). Return the arms back to your sides.

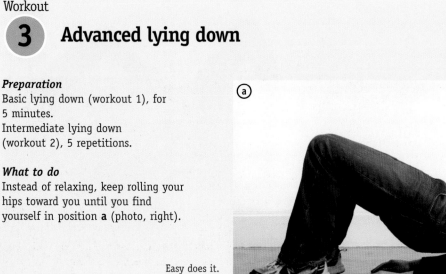

ⓐ Keep the waist and stomach muscles pulled in toward the spine, do not over-stretch.

ⓑ Keep control. Keep waist and stomach muscles pulled in toward the spine.

Try not to raise your shoulders.

Tip: Stand up slowly
Always get up slowly after floor exercises. Try to get a sense of maintaining the relaxation and power as you stand.

Stamina and flexibility

The next three workouts are designed to increase stamina and flexibility. Use these exercises to practice loosening up your inhibitions and letting go.

Tip: Set a time
Use a timer for these three exercises.

Workout

Baby in a buggy

Preparation
Lie down on your back with your legs and arms in the air.

Exercise
Imagine that you are a very happy and curious baby, desperate to explore your surroundings but too young to be able to move off of your back.

What to do
Move your arms, legs, and head in different directions. Reach for imaginary toys, grab your feet, try to turn around. Be spontaneous and energetic. The only rule is not to let your arms or legs touch the ground!

Basic position.

Reach in all directions.

Vary the pace to keep it feeling natural.

Duration
5 minutes.
Relax into actor lying down.

Help!
It hurts.
• If any of the exercises cause pain, stop immediately. Don't force anything. Aim to gradually build strength.

Workout

Rolling baby

Preparation
Baby in a buggy (workout 4)

What to do
Instead of relaxing, stretch out. Now roll one way onto your stomach. Keep going in the same direction until you are on your back again. Roll back onto your stomach and then onto your back.

Duration
Repeat 5 times as slowly as possible.
Relax into actor lying down.

Stretch out fully so that your shoulders are by your ears. This is a great exercise for loosening the shoulders.

Workout

Baby trying to crawl

Preparation
Baby in a buggy (workout 4).
Rolling baby (workout 5).

What to do
Instead of relaxing, roll onto your stomach. Keeping your torso connected with the floor at all times, pretend you are a baby trying to crawl but without the strength to lift yourself.

Duration
3 minutes.
Relax into actor lying down.

Move slowly and carefully at first. Don't strain the hip and shoulder joints.

What you want
To feel that the body is relaxed and balanced.

What you don't want
To feel tense.

Relaxation and posture

Now that you've worked on your posture lying down, it's time to learn how to re-create the same position standing up. The object here is to align the spine so that you can feel physically relaxed as you act. Relaxation is vitally important as there is a link between this and being emotionally open.

Workout

7 Neutral standing

Neutral standing is the starting position used by actors as a base for most vocal and movement exercises. It is also the essential canvas on which to build your characters, and is the basis for most workouts.

Preparation
Study the picture. Try standing in the same way. Make sure that your legs are straight but relaxed at the knees, with the feet and knees facing forward, hip width apart.

What to do
Slowly visualize your neck lengthening, your shoulders releasing, becoming more open and relaxed. Free up your back, eliminating additional tension. Now imagine that your body is being gently pulled up by an "invisible thread" (see below) attached to the top of your head. It should make you feel even more aligned, especially in the neck and shoulders.

Duration
1–5 minutes.

The invisible thread
To understand neutral standing, you have to get comfortable with the idea of the "invisible thread" (see above). Remember that whenever neutral standing is referred to in the book, it includes the invisible thread technique.

Workout

8 Rolling down the wall

Preparation
Put your back against the wall and then slide down until your knees are at right angles to the floor. Your back and shoulders are in contact with the wall (see picture, right).

What to do
Tuck the chin and gently roll downward, leading with the head, one vertebra at a time. Gently roll upward, one vertebra at a time. Leave the head till last.

Duration
Repeat 5 times.

Keep your shoulders square by making sure that your head is equally between both legs. Allow your arms to fall forward and your

shoulders and spine to totally relax. Imagine the back lengthening.

Neutral standing against a wall
This is the foundation for many of the workouts that follow. It is beneficial for you to get familiar with this basic starting position.

Stand naturally with your back and shoulder blades touching the wall. Look directly forward. There should be a slight gap between the back of your head and the wall.

Program 1: week 1

From Monday to Friday, for one week, follow either the "Program" or the "Mini Program." Remember to break off from this routine at weekends before moving onto Program 2 at the end of the next chapter. To achieve the best results, do the exercises recommended below as accurately as you can. Make time to do them properly without rushing.

Morning Session (30 minutes)

Workout 1
Basic lying down.

What to do:
Lie down in the basic lying down position.
Duration:
15 minutes.
Aim:
Release tension.

Workouts 4 and 5
Baby in a buggy/ Rolling baby.

What to do:
Baby in a buggy coming up into Rolling baby.
Duration:
Baby in a buggy for 3 minutes.

Rolling baby, 5 repetitions each way.
Aim:
Increase flexibility and strength.

Workout 7
Neutral standing.

What to do:
Study the neutral standing position (page 22).
Duration:
Stand and do a 5-minute visualization.
Aim:
Allow the body to become accustomed to the neutral standing position.

Evening Session (30 minutes)

Workout 3
Advanced lying down.

What to do:
10 minutes (instead of 5) of lying down before starting the movement.
Aim:
Release the tension of the day before working on strengthening the back.

Workouts 5 and 6
Rolling baby/Baby trying to crawl.

What to do:
5 slow repetitions of Rolling baby coming into 3 minutes of Baby trying to crawl.
Aim:
Increase strength, flexibility, and stamina.

Workout 8
Rolling down the wall.

What to do:
Gently roll up and down one vertebra at a time.
Duration:
3 slow repetitions.
Aim:
Balance and align the spine while standing.

Workout 7
Neutral standing.

What to do:
Repeat the morning's visualization exercise.
Duration:
5 minutes.
Aim:
Continue to educate your body posture.

Mini Program 1

Morning session (15 minutes)
Workout 1: Lie down in the basic lying down position for 15 minutes.

Evening session (15 minutes)
Workouts 4 and 5: Do Baby in a buggy coming up into Rolling baby.

Workout 7: Stand up and do a 5-minute visualization.

Don't forget!
Remember that your fitness program (pages 12–13) runs alongside the weekly program and continues until the end of the course.

To work in a naturally responsive way, you need to find a balance of freedom and control as you move. Once this is achieved you will discover that the body's muscles do much more than keep you upright and give you strength to perform actions. They possess what psychologists call a "sixth sense": a deeper level of movement capable of releasing and communicating emotion.

Chapter 2:
Movement

Where to begin

You need to find a sense of freedom and control in your movement. Like so much in acting, these things may seem like opposites but in fact they are not. Although the movement is free you are always aware of what you are doing. Therefore you have control.

> ***Neutral walking***
> Developing neutral walking as inspired by the Alexander Technique creates an excellent blank canvas on which to develop your character's movement. It lets gravity and alignment help you move more freely so you can focus on your performance.

Workout

9 Preparation for neutral walking 1

Preparation
Neutral standing against a wall (see workout 7).

Duration
Repeat 5 times.

What to do
Now slightly bend your legs, keeping back and shoulders against the wall and your feet flat on the ground (**a**). Slowly straighten your legs again and continue to rise onto the balls of your feet (**b**). Now back to neutral.

> ***Help!***
> I can't keep my balance.
> • Use the principle of the invisible thread (see neutral standing, workout 7) to help you balance.

Ⓐ

Keep your eyes focused directly ahead.

Ⓑ

Your heels rise off the floor as you push yourself up.

Workout

10 Preparation for neutral walking 2

✗

✓

Try not to lean forward, and don't tense the upper chest, shoulders, or neck.

Imagine the invisible thread when you are both bending and rising.

Preparation
Neutral standing against a wall (workout 7). Then take one step away from the wall.

Keep the focus directly forward.

What to do
Keeping your back in the same position as you were against the wall, bend your legs, while at the same time imagining the invisible thread (see workout 7). Straighten legs still imagining the thread pulling you upward. Now rise onto the balls of your feet. As you lower, imagine the thread still pulling your head up.

Duration
Repeat 5 times. Relax.

> ***Help!***
> Am I doing it correctly?
> • At the beginning of the workout it should feel as if your head is at exactly the same height from the ground even though your body is lowering. Keep practicing workout 9 to gain the necessary strength before you step away from the wall.

Workout

11 Neutral walking

(A)

Remember to remain balanced and relaxed.

(B)

Notice the positioning of the legs and feet.

Preparation
Neutral standing (workout 7) against a wall (remember the invisible thread).

What to do
Slowly bring your body forward so it leans in a straight line (**a**). Now take a step forward without leaning into the opposite hip (**b**).

Duration
Repeat a number of times with the right leg before starting with the left.

What you want
To feel that the momentum is taking you forward. It should feel natural to take a few more steps.

What you don't want
For your weight to pull you backward or sideways.

Help!
I don't understand.
• Remember, if you're going to step forward with the right leg, first of all you lean forward with your body in a straight line so that you've got the forward motion of gravity on your side. Now push directly ahead with the ball of the left foot as you raise the right leg to take a step.

Workout

12 Advanced walking

Preparation
Stand against the wall (workout 7). Imagine the thread lifting your head. Look forward.

What to do
Slowly allow your body to lean forward in a straight line. Now take a step without leaning into the opposite hip. Continue to walk around the room, knees and feet parallel, arms swinging gently from relaxed shoulders, head upright. Focus forward.

Once you have got the hang of advanced walking, take the posture outside for a stroll.

Tip: On the level
As you're walking, try to keep level. Don't rise and fall too much with each stride. As you get used to the exercise, the forward lean should be hardly noticeable.

Neutral walking: bad habits
When you take your step forward with your right leg, observe whether or not you lean your weight back onto your left heel. How about when you step forward with your left leg? Are you shifting your body weight onto your right heel?

This is a common mistake, but needs to be caught early and corrected as it restricts the energy of the walk. Make a point to be conscious of even subtle errors in your body posture.

Other movements

Now you have mastered standing and walking, it's time to explore other neutral movements too. Remember, at this stage it's all about balance and positioning.

Neutral sitting

Extra attention needs to be paid to the sitting position while acting. This is because, in real life, you usually sit down to rest and therefore, as an actor, you have to go against the body's natural urge to drop your energy. Learn these "tricks of the trade" to counteract this.

- Before sitting down, always stand directly in front of the chair (with your back to it) and pause. Doing this (while keeping it looking natural) prepares the audience for the movement, and keeps them focused.

- In order to maintain your energy while sitting, only sit on the front half of the chair. This makes it far easier for you to produce flowing work (it's also much easier to get up).

- If your character needs to lean or to slouch when sitting, then lean forward or sideways; never backward. Leaning backward makes you look lethargic and sends your energy to the back of the stage rather than out to the audience.

Tip: Be neutral
Many young actors lose a great deal of power in their performances because they sit, bend, or gesture in either an over-tense or over-relaxed way. This disrupts the flow of the energy you are creating.

Sitting badly or slouching can mean that your performance disappears to the back of the stage.

Energized and well balanced.

Workout

13

How to sit down

Preparation
Stand directly in front of the chair in a neutral standing position (see workout 7).

What to do
As you sit down, imagine the invisible thread pulling you up from the top of your head (see workout 7). Be sure to keep your back aligned, with knees and toes in line. Once seated take up a neutral sitting posture.

Duration
Practice a few times slowly. After that practice at a more naturalistic speed. Then practice walking to the chair and sitting. Don't forget to pause briefly before you sit.

Keep knees and toes parallel.

Workout

14 Standing up from a chair

Preparation
Sit neutrally on the chair (workout 13).

What to do
Place one leg slightly in front of the other. Lean your weight forward, without over-extending the lower spine. Push up with the legs to standing.

Duration
Repeat 5 times.

Allow gravity to pull you forward.

Workout

15 Moving the arms

Preparation
Neutral standing with your back and shoulders against a wall (see workout 7).

What to do
Raise both arms, keeping your shoulders relaxed and your back against the wall.

Duration
Repeat 10 times.

Allow the arms to float up. Don't focus on the shoulders.

Workout

16 Bending down

Preparation
Place a small object on the floor close to where you are standing. Stand neutrally (workout 7).

What to do
Now look at the object. Keeping your neck and back lengthened, bend down to pick it up.

Keep the neck and back long, and use the legs to take you closer to the floor.

Workout

17 A walk in the park 1

Preparation
Run through workouts 13–16.

What to do
Go for a stroll in the park. Study the people and natural world around you. Make a point of being really observant. Notice things that have never caught your eye before. When children are outdoors they instinctively combine walking, running, stopping, and sitting down. Do the same. Vary your physical actions and be playful.

Duration
15 minutes.

 What you want
To find a child-like freedom in yourself.

What you don't want
To pretend that you are actually a child.

Stage directions

Stage directions in the theater have stayed the same for hundreds of years. It is vital that you know what they mean so that you know where to go when instructed by the director. In your audition, the panel may choose to redirect your piece and are very likely to use these directions as instructions.

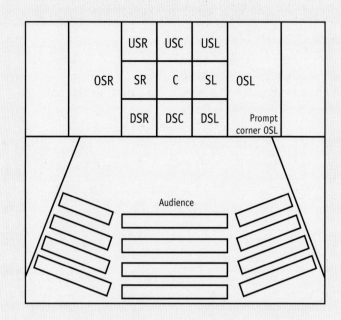

Upstage and Downstage

The theater stage was originally slanted (or raked) downward toward the stalls. This was so the actors at the back of the stage could be seen more clearly. This is why Downstage (DS) means walking toward the audience whereas Upstage (US) means walking toward the rear of the stage.

Stage Right and Stage Left

Imagine you are standing on the stage looking out into the audience. To your right is Stage Right (SR) and to your left is Stage Left (SL). If you are in the middle, you are standing Center Stage (C).

Prompt Corner is Off Stage Left (OSL) in the Downstage Corner. Originally, the prompter used to sit in this corner. Now it's nearly always the place the ASM (Assistant Stage Manager) sits to run the show.

KEY

Stage Right	SR
Stage Left	SL
Center Stage	C
Off Stage Right	OSR
Off Stage Left	OSL
Downstage	DS
Downstage Center	DSC
Upstage	US
Downstage Right	DSR
Downstage Left	DSL
Upstage Right	USR
Upstage Left	USL
Upstage Center	USC

Workout

  18 Basic stage directions

Preparation
Clear a space in a room. This is your stage. Establish where the audience are sitting and remind yourself of US, DS, SR, and SL. Place a cup OSL. Place a chair C. Sit on the chair.

What to do
Stand from C and walk DSL. Pause. Think about where you put the cup. Go OSR to look for it. Enter from OSR and stand behind chair C. Walk USC. Pause. Remember where you left the cup and hurry OSL to pick it up. Re-enter from L. Walk to Chair C. Sit. Pause. Think. Drink.

Aim
Practice neutral standing and moving (see workout 7 and workouts 13–16) while learning about the stage directions.

Workout

 19 Advanced stage directions

Enter from Prompt Corner. Take two steps SR, four steps US, three steps DSR, run USL and walk to USC. Walk DS slightly right of C to pick up an imaginary object. Think. Walk half a pace DSL and sit on the floor. You suddenly remember you have forgotten something. You run OSL (Downstage wing), OSL (Upstage wing), OSL (Downstage wing again) and then across to OSR (Downstage wing) where you find it. Enter slowly from OSR and sit happily on the floor.

Remembering your way around

These three stage workouts are designed to gradually increase in difficulty. Try them.

Recording your directions

A theater director needs to ensure that all the actors are standing in the right places at the right times. The director needs them to be able to be seen by the audience and also be in the correct position to interact with the other actors on the stage. It is a very complex process (especially considering that each actor might move hundreds of times during a single play). Actors must learn how to accurately record the stage movements given to them by their director. One missed move can wreck an entire scene.

Workout

20 Hitting your mark

Television and film work often involves "hitting the mark" (standing in a given spot that offers the camera the best possible angle) time and time again. This situation is trickier than it sounds (especially if you're running into shot!).

What to do
Invent your own stage direction nightmare that involves running into position to hit your mark.

Workout

21 Keeping level headed

Preparation
Place an empty plastic cup upside down on your head.

What to do
Repeat workouts 18 and 19 while balancing the cup.

Workout

22 Writing down stage directions

Preparation
Stand on your stage and make 10 moves in 10 different directions (e.g. 1 step US, 2 steps C, 5 quick baby steps toward OSL, etc.).

Repeat this 10-move pattern 3 times. The 10 moves should blur into a familiar and fluid pattern of movements.

What to do
Write down the stage directions for all the moves that you have been making.

Tip: Fill cup with water!
You need to make good posture look effortless. Balancing a cup or a book is great for acquiring steadiness and balance, essential skills when doing film and close-up TV shots. If you're feeling brave you can even turn over the cup and fill it with water!

Movement and the "method"

Konstantin Stanislavski (1863–1938) was a Russian actor and director working in the late 1800s. Unhappy with his own standard of acting he decided to develop a new technique of strongly internalized acting, the end result of which is more naturalistic performances.

A disciple of Stanislavski's, the Russian actor, director, and teacher Vsevolod Meyerhold, then took this method one step further into the physical world to create a new technique of physicalization called Biomechanics (or BM). His system of actor training teaches acting through purely physical work. It develops balance, coordination, flexibility, strength, and agility, and stresses that every physical movement communicates emotion, attitude, and the same inner, driving "need" that Stanislavski's method encouraged actors to explore internally.

Observing others

The next two pages encourage you as an actor to become more observant about the movement and physicality of others, something the method strongly encourages. An actor needs to be a great observer on stage as well as in everyday life.

"How can we teach unobservant people to notice what nature and life are trying to show them? First of all they must be taught to look at, listen to, and to hear what is beautiful. Such habits elevate their minds and arouse feelings which will leave deep traces in their emotion memories. Nothing in life is more beautiful than nature, and it should be the object of constant observation." Stanislavski, *An Actor Prepares*.

Careful observation of people is the key to injecting naturalistic movement and emotion into acting. Learn to notice how people run, jump, socialize and even relax—your work will be enriched by the number of observations you make.

Observational workouts

These exercises fall into two sections: internal and external. When observing internally you will be monitoring your body's physical tension. At the same time you should be open and aware of all that's going on around you. During the external observations you will be watching other people and noticing their movement, especially in relation to where they hold tension in their bodies. Do not stare, glare, judge, or take notes, please. Simply sit quietly with a book or a cup of coffee and naturally observe the people around you.

Workout
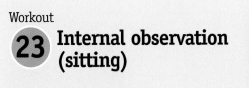 23 Internal observation (sitting)

Preparation
Go to a public place. Take a book.

Exercise
Internally observing yourself while sitting naturally and neutrally.

What to do
1. While you are reading, run a slow head to toe check on yourself. Become aware of any strain or tension in the body. If you notice tension, slightly alter your posture to achieve a more neutral sitting position (see workout 13). Imagine each part of your body relaxing. Allow the tension to disappear.

2. Allow the toes of both feet to relax, then the feet themselves, then the ankles. Move through the entire body until everything is relaxed and balanced.

Duration
15 minutes.

Help!
Nothing seems to be happening.
• Revisit Neutral sitting (workout 13) to remind yourself of the neutral sitting position. It may also help your alignment if you imagine the thread pulling from the top of your head.

What you want
Effortless alignment. Everything should flow naturally, even though you are sitting still in a public place. You should feel calm and relaxed. Be aware of those around you. This exercise should feel empowering.

What you don't want
To become so absorbed by the exercise that you become unaware of the other people around you.

Workout

External observation (sitting)

This exercise can lead directly on from workout 23 or can be done by itself.

Preparation
A public place.

What to do
As you people-watch, observe where other people store tension in their bodies, and how this affects their movements.

Duration
15 minutes.

Workout

25

Internal observation (standing/moving)

Preparation
Carry out this exercise in a public place either standing still or moving around the space.

What to do
Do an everyday chore (such as shopping) using only neutral movements. Notice where and when tension occurs in your body. See if you are able to make adjustments so that there is less strain in your body and you feel more energized.

Duration
30 minutes.

Help!
I can't correct the tension.
• It is more important at this stage to notice the tension rather than to correct it. Just take your posture back to neutral standing (see workout 7) or neutral walking (workout 11), and allow the tension to release on its own.

Workout

Film and television: watching the professionals

Nicole Kidman has a wonderful neck-line in front of the camera, as do actors such as Brad Pitt and George Clooney. Some great examples of a lack of tension in shoulders and neck can be found in Scarlett Johansen's performance in *Girl With a Pearl Earring* or Leonardo Di Caprio in *Titanic*.

Preparation
Rent a movie.

Exercise
Noticing lack of tension in shoulders and neck.

What to do
Watch the actors carefully. Notice how free they usually are in the shoulders and the neck area.

Duration
15 minutes.

.

Help!
Why do these actors seem so relaxed during their performances?
• Often they are trained to avoid the build-up of unnecessary tension in the body because this inhibits natural emotion. Even if an actor is playing a very angry character, he or she has to allow that emotion to flow through the body rather than attempt to contain it.

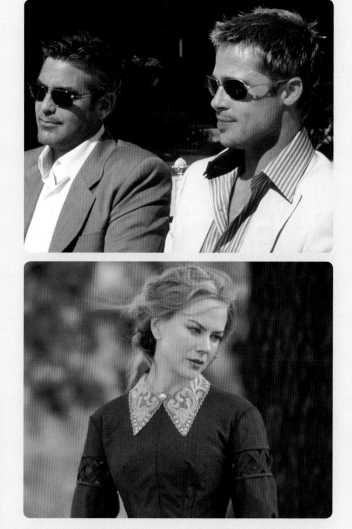

Top: Brad Pitt and George Clooney in *Ocean's 11*; above: Nicole Kidman in *Cold Mountain*.

Program 2: week 2

This program now replaces the old one and runs for the following week. You will also find that you will be incorporating some of the exercises into your daily routine. Some of the important workouts from Program 1 have been retained to establish a firm acting foundation.

Morning Session (45 minutes)

Workout 1
Basic lying down.

What to do:
Lie down in the basic lying down position.
Duration:
15 minutes.
Aim:
Release the tension in the body.

Workouts 4 and 5
Baby in a buggy/ Rolling baby.

What to do:
Baby in a buggy coming up into Rolling baby.
Duration:
Baby in a buggy for 3 minutes. Rolling baby 5 repetitions each way.
Aim:
Increase flexibility and strength.

Workout 7
Neutral standing.

What to do:
Study the neutral standing position.
Duration:
Stand and do a 5-minute visualization.
Aim:
Allow the body to become accustomed to the neutral standing position.

Workouts 9–11
Neutral walking.

Duration:
Repeat the exercise 5 times. Then take a break before repeating again.
Aim:
Strengthen your posture in preparation for movement.

Workout 10
Preparation for neutral walking 2.

Duration:
Repeat the exercise 5 times. Then take a break before repeating again.
Aim:
Continue to strengthen basic posture.

Everyday life

Workout 17
Go for a walk in the park twice a week to get the body used to neutral positioning.

Workouts 23–26
Choose from any of the observational exercises. Do at least three 15-minute sessions a week. This will help you become aware of unnecessary tension.

Evening Session (45 minutes)

Workout 3
Advanced lying down.

What to do:
Lie down in the basic lying down position.
Duration:
10 minutes (instead of 5) of lying down before starting the movement.
Aim:
Release the tension of the day before working on strengthening the back.

Workouts 5 and 6
Rolling baby/Baby trying to crawl.

Duration:
5 slow repetitions of Rolling baby coming into 3 minutes of Baby trying to crawl.
Aim:
Increase flexibility and strength.

Workout 8
Rolling down the wall.

What to do:
Gently roll up and down one vertebra at a time.
Duration:
3 slow repetitions.
Aim:
Balance and align the spine while standing.

Workout 9-17
Neutral movement.

What to do:
Choose any 3 of these exercises.
Duration:
Every day (Monday to Friday).
Aim:
Continue to educate the body in neutral movement.

Mini Program 2

Morning session (15 minutes)

Workout 1
Lie down in the basic position for 15 minutes.

Everyday life (15 minutes)

Workout 17
Walk in the park. Two times in the week.

Workouts 23-26
Choose 3 observational exercises each week.

Evening session (15 minutes)

Workouts 9-17
Choose 2 per day.

We talk every day, but when we do we often have to hide our true feelings. This has a restricting effect on our voices. We have to learn to be free again; to get rid of strange habits and artificial patterns. Just think: If a baby can scream for hours without its voice wearing out, then so can we. This is not about learning a new skill; it's simply about remembering an old one.

Chapter 3: Voice

The importance of the voice

The voice is by far the most important tool at an actor's disposal.

If you injure an arm or a leg, it is usually possible to adapt your performance accordingly so the show can go on. If you injure your voice, however, nothing can be done. This can have a devastating effect on the success of the production. Without vocal training, your voice may be "trapped" in certain inflexible or artificial patterns. This can have a destructive effect on your performance because, although the audience may be able to hear and understand you, you will not be able to engage freely with your character, or convey your emotions truthfully.

If working on a movie, an untrained voice is a liability. If your voice becomes inconsistent, it makes continuity a problem. There is much expected of an actor's vocal equipment, so it must be well trained and extremely well cared for. In the same way that world-class musicians merge with the music that they play, you do not notice the technique behind the delivery of a great actor, as he or she becomes one with the character.

About your vocal equipment

If you try lifting a heavy object, you will notice that you hold a type of "pressure blockage" in your throat. Surprisingly, lifting (along with eating and drinking) is one of the main reasons for the natural design of the vocal apparatus. It implies that any sort of tension can have a negative "blocking" effect on voice production.

Looking after the voice

What you want to do
- *The voice should float on the breath, supported by the diaphragm.*
- *Drink warm water to occasionally soothe the vocal cords.*

What you don't want to do
- *Shout too much.*
- *Drink too much alcohol or caffeine.*
- *Eat too much chocolate or dairy.*
- *Drink too many ice-cold drinks.*
- *Stay close to heating systems that will dry out your throat.*

The journey of the breath

Let's trace the journey of the breath through the body. As you breathe out, exhalation causes sound to vibrate through the vocal cords of the throat and in the chest, mouth, and head cavities. After that, the required sounds are formed and articulated.

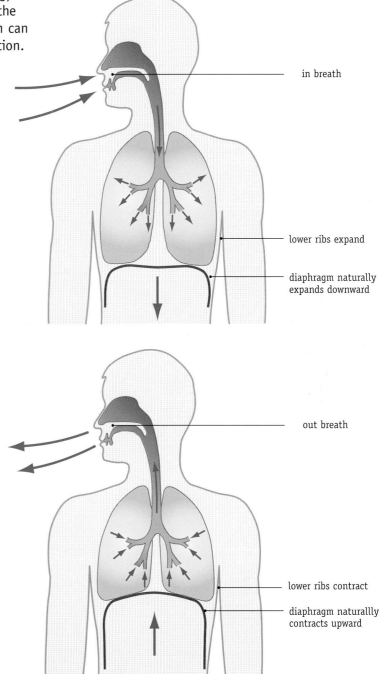

in breath

lower ribs expand

diaphragm naturally expands downward

out breath

lower ribs contract

diaphragm naturallly contracts upward

Foundation for the voice
Good breathing technique will support the voice and allow you to perform effortlessly. If you study and practice the breathing exercises in this book diligently, your breathing will become natural and unconscious, allowing you to progress in your acting work.

Controlling the breath

Breathing has a natural, subconscious rhythm. This is the case because we breathe to live— we don't even think about it. As an actor, you need to study this natural rhythm, and get in contact with its patterns and behavior. Only then can you strengthen and adapt your breathing apparatus to meet your needs as an actor.

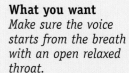

What you want
Make sure the voice starts from the breath with an open relaxed throat.

What you don't want
For the voice to start in the throat.

Workout
27 Natural breathing patterns

Preparation
Basic lying down (workout 1).

What to do
Observe your breathing without changing it. Notice whether your chest or stomach rises or falls.

Always work carefully and gently. Easy does it.

Duration
10 minutes.

Keep your eyes closed and feel the movement of the breath from inside the body.

Workout
28 Neutral tongue and throat

To discourage tension, it is important to relax the throat and correctly place the tongue while breathing.

Preparation
Neutral standing (workout 7).

Shoulders and neck are balanced and relaxed. The eyeline is forward. The tongue is flat with the tongue tip touching the base of the lower teeth.

What to do
Keep the throat open and relaxed with the tongue relaxed and flat against the base of the mouth. Make sure the shoulders stay completely relaxed. Breathe in through the nose for a count of 10. Breathe out through the mouth for a count of 10.

Duration
Repeat 5 times.

How to breathe (for actors)

Notice that the shoulders and the upper chest remain relaxed and still, while the stomach and waist stay firm and strong. All the work happens in the lower ribs and diaphragm. Sometimes this technique is called "breathing from the stomach." This can be very misleading. Ideally, the stomach muscles should move very little. Make sure your breathing is silent.

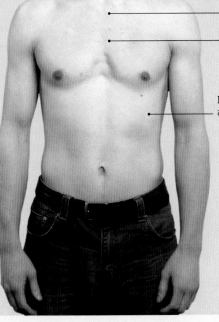

Beginning of the in breath

End of the out breath

Upper chest relaxed.

Chest and spine balanced in neutral standing.

Lower rib cage relaxed and expanding.

Lower rib cage contracting.

Waist and stomach muscles in toward spine.

Core energy

The breath energy starts in the lower ribs and diaphragm. The rest of the body is relaxed, balanced, and neutral. This natural breathing through a balanced, relaxed body is what allows the acting to flow smoothly.

Workout

29 Correct breathing while standing

Preparation
Neutral standing (see workout 7).

What to do
Relax shoulders and upper chest. Place hands on your lower ribs. As you breathe in, extend the lower ribs and apply gentle pressure with the hands to give the ribs something to push against (this will help you feel the movement more easily).

Duration
Repeat 10 times.

Hands on ribs in contracted position.

Help!
Nothing is moving.
- This is a difficult exercise for any beginner. At an early stage it may help to clench your stomach muscles. This makes any movement of the lower ribs easier to detect. Avoid tensing shoulders or upper chest.

Hands on ribs in extended position.

The hands should be pushed outward on the "in" breath, and should return to your starting point on the "out" breath. This will strengthen the diaphragm and extend the lower ribs.

Workout

30 Correct breathing lying down

Preparation
Basic lying down (see workout 1).
Pull your waist and stomach muscles toward the spine. This exercise strengthens the diaphragm and extends the lower ribs. Try to keep a neutral tongue and throat (see workout 28).

What to do
While keeping the shoulders and upper chest relaxed, place one hand on the navel. Take a shallow breath in and expand the lower ribs. Don't allow the hand on the navel to rise or fall. Breathe in for a count of 10. Breathe out for a count of 10.

Duration
Repeat 10 times, gradually deepening and slowing the breath a little more each time.

Help!
When the air rushes in my upper chest expands.
• This is a natural body response. Practice expanding the lower ribs in the earlier exercises in order to eventually achieve total relaxation in the upper chest.

Workout

31 Advanced breathing lying down

Preparation
Basic lying down (see workout 1).

What to do
While keeping the shoulders and upper chest relaxed, with the waist and stomach muscles pulled inward toward the spine, place one hand on the navel and the other on the upper chest. Take a breath in and out, trying not to allow either of the hands to rise or fall. All the movement should happen from the lower ribs only.

Duration
Repeat 10 times, gradually deepening the breath each time.

When to control and when not to control
It is important at the early stages of breathing work not to hold your breath when the lungs are full. This creates tension and pressure in the throat, and you want the throat to remain open and relaxed. This next exercise uses the body's natural reflex system to ensure that your breathing remains powerful without building any unnecessary pressure.

Workout

32 Spontaneous breathing 1

Preparation
Basic lying down (see workout 1). As with workout 31, keep your shoulders and upper chest relaxed, and place one hand on the navel and the other on the upper chest. Take a breath in.

What to do
Breathe out for a count of 10. Now wait for a count of 10 with empty lungs. Then open your throat and allow the air to naturally rush in, filling the lungs. Slowly breathe out for a count of 10.

Duration
Repeat 3 times.

Workout

33 Spontaneous breathing 2

Preparation
Neutral sitting (workout 13).

What to do
Position three lit candles on the table in front of you: one at 4 in (10cm) from your face, the next at 12 in (30cm), and the last at 20 in (50cm). Keeping the shoulders and the neck relaxed, and shaping the mouth into an "oo" shape, use the diaphragm to blow out the three candles, one at a time, in short bursts of breath.

Duration
Once you have blown the three candles out, rest.
Repeat 5 times (no more).

Workout

34 Adding sound to spontaneous breathing 1

Preparation
Basic lying down (see workout 1).

What to do
As with workout 32, keep your shoulders and upper chest relaxed, and place one hand on the navel and the other on the upper chest. Take a breath "in," trying not to allow either of the hands to rise or fall. Keep a neutral tongue and throat. You should be as relaxed as possible. Very gently hum on the "out" breath until the lungs are empty. Hum with the lips pressed together so you feel a vibration on them. Inhale and repeat.

Duration
Repeat 5 times.

Your head should feel balanced on your neck.

Face forward, shoulders relaxed, elongated neck.

Workout

35 Adding sound to spontaneous breathing 2

Preparation
Neutral standing against a wall (workout 7).

What to do
Keep your shoulders, neck, face, and upper chest relaxed. Keep a neutral tongue and throat. Take a deep breath in and gently hum. When the lungs are empty, expand the lower ribs and allow a deep breath in.

Duration
Repeat 5 times.

 What you want
You should begin to feel the lower ribs expanding with a sense of strength, power, and control.

What you don't want
To control the hum with the throat. When you first do this exercise the hum should be very uneven.

Workout

36 Walk in the park 2

Preparation
Neutral walking (workouts 9–11).

What to do
Go for a walk. Repeat workout 35 but this time walk rather than stand. Hold your arms naturally by your sides rather than on your ribs.

Duration
3 x 5 minute repetitions with a 3-minute rest in between each.

Resonating, not projecting

Projecting your voice is important, but you need to project *yourself* if you are going to connect with an audition panel.

The audition panel really need to see who you are; really feel what you're feeling—even with character work, they do not want to see someone pretending to be someone else. They want to see a real person in that particular situation; and this is where resonance comes into play.

So how do you project yourself? Well, imagine a gong. When hit, it vibrates the air around it, producing sound waves. Now, imagine yourself as an instrument. If you vibrate then the sound waves project you! If you are feeling a certain emotion then this will be projected through your resonance, without effort.

In the audition you want to make the truth bigger. You want to reach every member of the panel on an emotional level and draw them into your work. This is very different to projecting at them. Learning this skill makes an actor versatile. So try to resonate with the whole truth, rather than projecting in a shallow way.

Traditional approaches
Theater leading up to the late 1800s was all about detachment from real feelings, with performances being "acted" rather than felt. But we have long moved past this; even the slightest hint of falseness in your audition will send you heading for the exit.

What you want
To be able to feel your voice.

What you don't want
To leave your emotions behind when you speak.

Tip: Let it vibrate
If you want your performances to hit the back of a large theater, if you want your movie work to be truthful, quiet, and intense, then you need to learn how to resonate. Your body literally needs to vibrate with the truth.

With the resonance exercises you have to allow the sound to find where it's meant to be. It takes patience, so be gentle, and start slowly. If you force the resonance it will produce a loud voice that is not flexible and therefore not suitable for TV or movie work.

Workout 37 — Humming exercise for the facial cavities

Preparation
Neutral standing (workout 7, page 22).

What to do
1 Gently hum. Smile the sound into the cheeks.
Duration
1 minute.

2 Raise your eyebrows so that the sound goes into the forehead.
Duration
1 minute.

3 Continue to hum with a relaxed face.
Duration
1 minute.

Am I getting it right?
When the face is relaxed in step 3, you should feel the sensation in both the cheeks and forehead.

Help!
Make sure that there is no tension. Keep a neutral tongue and throat (see workout 28, page 42).

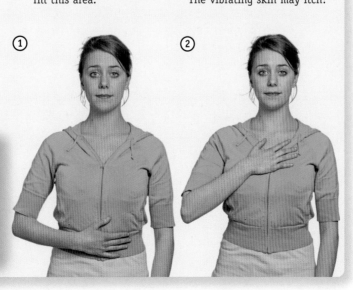

① ② ③

Workout 38 — Resonating the body cavities

Preparation
Neutral standing (workout 7).

What to do
1 Place your hand just below the solar plexus. Gently hum. Allow the sound to vibrate in this area.

Duration
1 minute.

2 Place your hand onto your upper chest. Gently hum. Allow the vibration to fill this area.

Duration
1 minute.

Am I getting it right?
It should feel gentle, like a very light internal massage. The vibrating skin may itch!

① ②

Help!
If you can't feel the vibration simply imagine the sound going to the correct places.

Workout 39 — Walk in the park 3

Preparation
Walk in the park (workout 36).

What to do
Repeat workout 36, and add the humming from workout 37.

Duration
15 minutes.

Vowels and consonants

While the consonant sounds add sharpness and clarity to the words spoken on the stage or screen, the vowel sounds convey the emotion within the writer's words. Vowels are longer, more open sounds, connected directly to the breath. The breath, in turn, is connected to the emotions.

Vowels
The vowels are "a, e, i, o, u," and all possible combinations of these letters when spoken aloud.

Consonants
The consonants are the other 21 letters of the alphabet. The consonant sounds are harder (and usually shorter) than the vowel sounds, and are all the possible combinations of the consonants when spoken aloud.

Take the word "start," for example. The sound of the first letter is "sss." If you repeat this "sss" you will sound something like a hissing snake. It is a hard, inflexible sound and it is very difficult to convey any sort of variation of emotion with it. It doesn't matter whether you try to be a happy snake or a sad snake; the chances are that your hiss will sound more or less the same as every other hiss.

The vowel sound in the middle of "start" is "ar," which is often written in voice work as "ah." This is a very flexible, open sound. "Ah" can be expressed in a number of different ways. For example, you can use it as if you are in pain, or as if you have just seen a newborn baby. In each case, the emotion will cause the sound to be different.

How the vowel sounds are made

Basic vowel sounds are made by changing the positioning of the tongue and the lips around one basic shape: "ah."

"Ah"
as in start

"Or"
as in four

"Oo"
as in moon

Place the mouth in the open "ah" shape. Move the lips forward and close them slightly.

Keep a neutral tongue and throat. The mouth is open and the lips are pushing ever so slightly forward.

Again, exactly as with "ah." This time the lips are pouted even further forward. The mouth remains open in the "ah" shape.

Workout

40 Silent vowel positions 1: ah, or, oo

Preparation
Neutral standing (workout 7). Study the "ah, or, oo" mouth positions on page 49.

What to do
Look into a mirror. Open your mouth into the "ah" position (with a neutrally relaxed tongue). Without moving the jaw or tongue move the lips to the "or" position, then finally to "oo."

Duration
Repeat each 20 times. Look in a mirror for the first 10 repetitions. Close your eyes for the last 10.

Workout

41 Silent vowel positions 2: ah, ae, ee

Preparation
Neutral standing (workout 7). Study the "ah, ae, ee" mouth positions opposite.

What to do
Look into a mirror. Open your mouth into the "ah" position (with a neutrally relaxed tongue). Without moving the jaw or tongue move the lips to the "ae" position, then finally to "ee."

Duration
Repeat each 20 times. Look in a mirror for the first 10 repetitions. Close your eyes for the last 10.

"ah"

Mouth is in the open "ah" shape (see previous page).

"ae"

"Ae" as in hay.
With the mouth in the "ah" shape, and the tongue tip resting against the bottom teeth, raise the body of the tongue. Slightly widen the mouth.

"ee"

"Ee" as in teeth.
From the "ae" position, raise the tongue still further and stretch the lips wider. As you widen the shape, the teeth will naturally come closer together.

Connecting the vowel sounds to the breath

Connecting the voice to the breath may seem like a straight forward process. However, many new actors produce the voice almost entirely from the throat with little breath support, rather than floating the voice on the breath. This constricts the voice and over-complicates it. These next exercises will help you simplify things.

Workout

 42 ## Connecting the vowel sounds to the hum 1

Preparation
Neutral standing (see workout 7).

What to do
Keep shoulders and neck relaxed. Take a deep breath in. Connect the out breath to a hum. Now, without breaking the sound, push your lips forward into the "oo" shape, making the "oo" sound. Relax.

Duration
Repeat 5 times.

Help!
I don't understand the sequence of sounds.
• Here is the sound of the exercise written down:

"HHHMMMM MMMOOOOOO OOOOOOOOO."

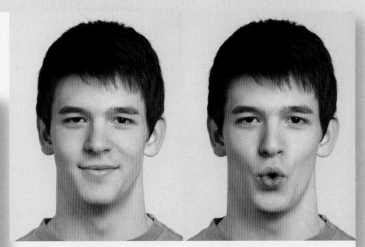

Humming.   Lips forward to "oo."

Tip: Keep it quiet and gentle
The hum moves effortlessly into the "oo" sound by pushing the lips forward. Make sure the sound is connected to the breath.

Workout

 43 ## Connecting the vowel sounds to the hum 2

Preparation
Neutral standing(see workout 7).

What to do
Start with the hum and move into the "oo" sound (exactly as in workout 42). On the second repetition, move the mouth from the hum into the "or" sound instead. Then, for the third, fourth, and fifth repetitions, move from the hum into "ah," then "ae," and finally "ee."

Duration
Repeat each sound 5 times.

Help!
I am unsure about the sequence.
• The exercise looks like this:
"HHHMMMMMMOO" (holding the "oo" until the end of the breath). 5 times.
"HHHMMMMMMOR" (holding the "or" until the end of the breath). 5 times.
"HHHMMMMMMAH" etc.
"HHHMMMMMMAE" etc.
"HHHMMMMMMEE" etc.

Tip: Use a mirror
Check your positioning in the mirror on a regular basis. Remember to go easy. The sound should be effortless and relaxed.

Working the consonants

Consonants add clarity, sharpness, and attack to your speech. Working with these kinds of consonant-heavy tongue twisters energizes and frees your mouth and tongue.

Tongue twisters

This type of vocal exercise is meant to be difficult to say. Here are three tongue twisters guaranteed to get your mouth moving.

Workout

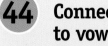 Connecting consonant sounds to vowel sounds

Preparation
Neutral standing (workout 7).
Remind yourself of the vowel sequence: "oo, or, ah, ae, ee." (see page 51)

What to do
This exercise involves repeating the sequence, but this time with consonants in front of the vowel sounds:

"BOO, BOR, BAH, BAE, BEE
DOO, DOR, DAH, DAE, DEE,
FOO, FOR, FAR, FAE, FEE,
GOO, GOR, GAH, GAE, GEE"

Carry on the pattern using the rest of the alphabet. Now try adding these to the basic vowel sounds:

"CH, CL, PR, SH, ST."

Help!
I find learning lines difficult.
• Just learn two lines a day. Then build to four lines a day. Gradually increase the linage. After a few months of dedicated practice your line learning will become effortless (learning lines is an important skill to develop if you want to be an actor).

Workout

 Tongue twister 1

Preparation
Neutral standing.

What to do
Repeat this verse:

"BETTY BOTTER BOUGHT SOME BUTTER
BUT SHE SAID THE BUTTER'S BITTER
IF I PUT IT IN MY BATTER
IT WILL MAKE MY BATTER BITTER
BUT A BIT OF BETTER BUTTER'S
BOUND TO MAKE MY BATTER BETTER
SO SHE BOUGHT A BIT OF BUTTER
BETTER THAN HER BITTER BUTTER
AND SHE PUT IT IN HER BATTER
AND IT MADE HER BATTER BETTER
SO A BIT OF BETTER BUTTER'S
BETTER FOR A BITTER BATTER."

Tip
Don't allow tension into any part of the body (especially shoulders and neck).

Workout

46 **Tongue twister 2**

Try this verse:

"SHE SELLS SEA SHELLS ON THE SEA SHORE
WHERE SHE SAW SIX SICK SHEEP
ON THE SEA SHORE'S SEE-SAW."

Workout

47 **Tongue twister 3**

Try this verse:

"TARA PALMER-TOMKINSON TALKED
ABOUT THE TIP OF THE TONGUE, THE
TEETH, AND THE LIPS."

Troubleshooting

The exercises on these two pages are excellent workouts in their own right. They focus on the two main areas that usually require extra attention for anyone aspiring to train as an actor: a slow-moving mouth (poor enunciation), and tension in the shoulders and neck causing the actor to speak from the throat rather than by using the power of the breath.

Problem: A lazy mouth

When the mouth is not moved enough, the sound produced is dull and under-energized. This may be caused by shyness, or lazy diction. Workouts 48 and 49 are two different exercises to get your mouth moving.

Workout 48 — Energizing the mouth 1

Preparation
Neutral standing (workout 7).

What to do
Make your finger into the shape shown in the detail below. Place the finger into your mouth. Repeat the tongue twister in workout 45 (page 52) with your finger in your mouth.

Duration
Repeat once.

Repeat workout 45 without the finger.

Help!
I can't pronounce the words.
• The aim of the exercise is to get the mouth moving. You are not meant to be able to pronounce the words properly with your finger in your mouth. Simply pronounce the words as best you can, breathe correctly, and relax your shoulders. The sound starts with the breath.

Do not bite onto your finger. It is just a guide to help keep your mouth open. If your mouth doesn't open this wide, turn the finger sideways.

Workout 49 — Energizing the mouth 2

Preparation
Neutral standing (see workout 7).

What to do
Stick your tongue out. Now allow it to relax. Grab hold of it gently. Do not pull the tongue—the hold is just a guide to keep the tongue out of the way. Repeat workout 45 (page 52) in this position.

Duration
Repeat once.

Repeat workout 45 as normal.

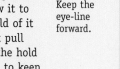
Keep the eye-line forward.

Allow the tongue to relax out of the mouth.

Hold the tip of the tongue. Do not hold tightly.

Problem: Tension and breath errors

Many young actors start out with a noticeable amount of tension in the neck and shoulders. This restricts the movement of the jaw and encourages speech from the throat rather than speech that is supported by breath.

Speaking from the throat not only creates a hard, inflexible sound but using this area indefinitely can also be dangerous (it can lead to all sorts of physical problems within the vocal mechanism). This is especially true if you are forcing the voice by speaking loudly on stage. Vocal work should be like a caress, with the breath simply stroking the vocal cords.

Workout

51 Energizing speech with resonance

Preparation
Neutral standing (see workout 7).
Repeat workout 37.
Repeat workout 38.

Repeat workout 45 again, focusing on the body. Relax.

Duration
2 repetitions.

What to do
Repeat workout 45, focusing on resonating in the facial cavities.

Relaxed and balanced.

Visible tension in the upper neck.

Workout

50 Energizing speech without tension

Preparation
Memorize the first four lines of a tongue twister in workouts 45–47. Lie down in the basic lying down position (page 18). Focus on keeping your neck relaxed.

What to do
Speak the lines very slowly and very clearly, constantly making sure that your neck stays totally relaxed.

Duration
Repeat 5 times.

Program 3: week 3

It's week three, replace Program 2 with Program 3. The work is becoming more intense, so make sure that you hold your focus and keep your eye on the goal. Remember, if you're short of time, you could follow the Mini Program.

Morning Session (50 minutes)

Workout 1
Basic lying down.

Duration:
15 minutes.
Aim:
Release the tension.

Workouts 4 and 5
Baby in a buggy and Rolling baby.

What to do:
Start the exercise in Baby in a buggy and go directly into Rolling baby.
Duration:
Baby in a buggy:
3 minutes.
Rolling baby:
5 repetitions each way.
Aim:
Increase flexibility and strength.

Workouts 34 and 35
Adding sound to breath.

Duration:
Do 10 repetitions of each workout. Take a short break between each in basic lying down.
Aim:
Strengthen the breath and connect it to sound.

Workout 10
Preparation for neutral walking 2.

Duration:
Repeat the exercise 5 times. Take a break before repeating again.
Aim:
Strengthen your basic posture.

Workouts 37 and 38
Resonating the voice.

Duration:
Repeat each workout on 5 breaths.
Aim:
To increase vocal resonance.

Everyday Life

Workout 17
Walk in the park 1.
What to do:
Go for a walk in the park twice a week to get the body used to neutral positioning.

Workout 39
Walk in the park 3.

What to do:
Do this workout for 15 minutes, twice a week. This will strengthen your vocal resonance.

Workouts 23-26
Observational workouts.

What to do:
Choose one workout from 23-26 and do it twice a week. These observational exercises will help you become aware of tension in yourself and others.

Evening Session (45 minutes)

Workout 3
Advanced lying down.

Duration:
10 minutes (instead of 5) of lying down before starting the movement.
Aim:
Release the tension of the day before working on strengthening the back.

Workouts 5 and 6
Rolling baby and Baby trying to crawl.

What to do:
Start the exercise in Rolling baby and go directly into Baby trying to crawl.
Duration:
Rolling baby:
5 slow repetitions.
Baby trying to crawl:
3 minutes.
Aim:
Increase flexibility and strength.

Workout 8
Rolling down the wall.

Duration:
3 slow repetitions.
Aim:
To balance and align the spine while standing.

Workout 33
Spontaneous breathing 2.

Duration:
Repeat 5 times. Take a rest in between.
Aim:
To strengthen the diaphragm.

Workout 43
Connecting vowel sounds to the hum 2.

Duration:
Repeat 5 times.
Aim:
To connect the vowel sounds to the breath.

Workout 44
Connecting consonant sounds to vowel sounds.

Duration:
1 repetition.
Aim:
Strengthen the consonant sounds.

Workouts 48 and 49
Energizing the mouth.

What to do:
Repeat the tongue twisters as a sequence in the following manner:
• with your finger in your mouth.
• holding the tongue.
• speaking normally.
Duration:
Repeat the above sequence twice.
Aim:
Energize and free the mouth.

Workout 50
Energizing speech without tension.

Duration:
5 times.
Aim:
Strengthen the connection between voice and breath.

Mini Program 3

Workout 1
Basic lying down:
5 minutes.

Workout 3
Advanced lying down:
Repeat this workout for 10 minutes.

Evening session (15 minutes)
Workouts 46 and 47
Repeat each tongue twister once through with a finger in your mouth. Repeat each tongue twister once through holding your tongue. Repeat each tongue twister once through normally.

Everyday life Workout 17
Walk in the park once a week.
Workout 39
Walk in the park 3:
15 minutes. Twice a week.

Workouts 23-26
Observational workouts:
Choose one workout from 23-26.
Do it twice a week.

Most acting schools judge you on your ability to perform a given speech. You need to lift the words from the page and give them life. Remember, this is what an actor does for a living. Being able to improvise is one thing, but acting from a script is the basis of nearly all TV, film, and theater work.

Chapter 4:
Performing Text

Audition requirements

Most theater schools will ask you to prepare at least two contrasting pieces of text for your audition. This is so they can assess:

How well you can "hold" the performance space on your own.

Do you have the confidence to hold the audience's complete focus when on stage? How much life and energy can you bring to your performance? Are you able to convey the kind of authenticity that makes audiences want to watch your every move?

How well you can bring "emotional truth" to your work.

Can you place yourself truthfully and emotionally in your character's shoes? Are you able to share this emotion with your audience?

Your ability to exist "in the moment."

How spontaneous does your performance look and feel? Are you able to act as if this is the first time your character has said these words and felt these feelings? Do you believe that the environment you have created around you is real?

Your ability to understand "text in context."

Events in a play provide clues about how to act your particular piece of text. What has your character said and done up to that point? What do they say and do afterward? What is done to them? What is the playwright's intention for the piece? In what period of history and social situation is the text set?

5 **Your ability to "characterize" a piece of text.**

Can you play a character that is a "real" person and not a stereotype or a cliché? Can you make your movement and vocal skills completely convincing?

6 **Your capacity for "theatrical awareness."**

Do you have a sense of how to "be" on the stage? Are you able to imagine the presence of the characters mentioned in your monologue? Do you seem like a "natural"?

7 **Your capacity for "theatrical intelligence."**

Have you set your pieces effectively? Does your character move from one place to the other at the right moment and in the appropriate way?

8 **Your ability to work in both comic and tragic roles.**

Do you have a significant understanding of how comedy and tragedy work? Do you know the difference between the two?

Focus and truth

Rehearsing is a very different activity from performing live. The public has a strong effect on the actor, who can get over-enthusiastic (as if controlled by the performance), or numbed (as if in shock). To avoid this, here are some exercises for you to practice holding your concentration and focus on stage.

Workout

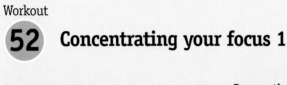 **Concentrating your focus 1**

 What you want
You should find that you become less self-conscious as the exercise progresses. The world around you will seem to disappear because you are concentrating.

What you don't want
To tense up as you concentrate.

Preparation
Neutral sitting (workout 13).

What to do
Hold an object in your hand. Examine it closely. Really look at every minute detail.

Duration
5 minutes.

Relax into the exercise.

Workout

53 Concentrating your focus 2

 What you want
What you should find is that your voice becomes freer. Instead of focusing on how your voice sounds—by listening to yourself—you are focusing on the physical object instead, to take your mind off your speech. This will help you become more vocally truthful and flexible. So, in the performance space, by focusing on an object on the stage, it is possible to free your voice and give a more truthful performance.

What you don't want
Don't focus so hard that you give yourself eye strain. Keep it natural.

Preparation
Neutral sitting (workout 13).

What to do
Focus on an object in the room about 7ft (2m) away from you. Really look at it and examine it in every detail.

Duration
Repeat each tongue twister (see workouts 45–47) while continuing to explore the detail of the object.

Don't think about the words, just allow them to come out naturally.

Workout

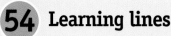

54 Learning lines

Preparation
Pick a short poem no more than six lines long (try Rainer Maria Rilke's "Time and Again" if you are stuck).

What to do
Learn one line a day, every day, for a week. On the seventh day, repeat the whole poem to yourself, over and over again. The next week, progress to a longer poem (try Shakespeare's Sonnet 18) and learn two to three lines per day. Keep working this way with a different longer poem every time.

Tip: Try paraphrasing
When you get good at memorizing lines there are other, more organic, ways to learn a script. Get the gist of the piece by paraphrasing the part or learn the lines in association with your stage movements.

Workout

55 Freeing emotional truth 1

Preparation
Neutral standing (workout 7).
Place an object in the room about 13ft (4m) away from you. Make sure that the object has some kind of emotional meaning to you (perhaps a ring, or a gift).

What to do
Focus on that object, allowing your natural feeling to emerge. Repeat the tongue twisters in workouts 45–47 while holding focus.

Duration
Repeat each tongue twister once.

Help!
There's too much for me to remember.
• Just make sure you know your lines. Let everything else arrive at its own pace.

 What you want
Not only should the voice be free but the emotion should naturally affect the words without you thinking about it. Focus on the object, not the words you are speaking.

What you don't want
To force the emotion in any way. Just allow it to emerge.

Finding emotional truth
An actor can't emotionally move an audience with technique alone. To play the truth means to "think, strive, feel, and act in unison with your role," as Stanislavski said. He developed something he called the "magic if." In terms of emotional truth, the "magic if" means that the actor must act as if they truly are in that situation. For example, if you are playing a homeless character, you don't just act like a homeless person, you must play the character as "if" you are really in that situation.

Workout

56 Freeing emotional truth 2

Preparation
Looking out of the window.

What to do
Focus on something in the distance. While focusing, think of a funny moment. Repeat each tongue twister (workouts 45–47) while in that emotional state.

Duration
Repeat each tongue twister once.

Tip: Comic acting
Dramatic emotions are often easier to find than comic ones. You may need to inject a little more energy.

Workout

57 Freeing emotional truth 3

Preparation
Remind yourself of workout 56 (above).

What to do
Repeat workout 56. Instead of thinking of a funny moment, think of a sad moment.

Duration
Repeat each tongue twister once.

Being "in the moment"

Stanislavski described acting as "the art of living the part," or what can also be described as "being in the moment." Being in the moment requires you to be so entirely focused and relaxed that the subconscious mind feels safe to work without being put off by its surroundings. To promote this focus, Stanislavski developed a system that he called "circles of attention."

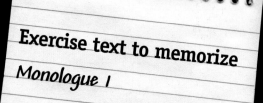

Exercise text to memorize

Monologue 1

"Jack should not be friends with Brian. Those two are real trouble, I tell you. What they did yesterday was beyond a joke. I mean, they're nearly 17 and yet they act like they're 10 or 11 years old."

Workout

58 Small circle of attention (sitting 1)

Preparation
Neutral sitting (workout 13) in a darkened room next to a lamp that is switched off. Memorize monologue 1.

What to do
Turn on the lamp. Notice the small area of light. Look in minute detail at what is lit. Look at your hands in the light and examine them in detail. Notice how dark it is outside the lit area. Using this small circle of attention, recite monologue 1 (above). Make sure you use the small and cozy area to feel intimate and safe.

Duration
Repeat once.

Moving the circle

Your small circle of attention can be very useful in nerve-racking situations such as auditions. The next stage is to be able to move around while maintaining the focus.

59 Small circle of attention (sitting 2)

Preparation
Remind yourself of workout 58.

Duration
1 repetition

What to do
Recreate the atmosphere of workout 58, but with all the lights switched on.

Workout

60 Small circle of attention (moving)

Preparation
Fill a bowl with water.

What to do
Focus on the level of the water in the bowl. Pick up the bowl and carry it very slowly from one side of the room to the other. Make sure you don't spill a drop.

Duration
2 minutes.
In the second minute, as you are walking, repeat monologue 1 (opposite).

Medium and large circles of attention

While small circles of attention are used to draw an audience in, medium and large circles of attention are used by actors to reach out to their audience. The entire point of developing your craft is to share your work with others. According to Stanislavski: "To create the life of a human spirit and to express it in a beautiful artistic form (is the goal of the actor)." In other words, although stage performances seem naturalistic and employ natural emotion, they are still technically masterful.

Workout

61 Medium circle of attention

Preparation
Sitting in a dark room.

What to do
Turn on the lights. Imagine the darkness outside of the room. Repeat monologue 1 (opposite).
Be aware of your circle of attention expanding to fill the lit space.

Duration
Repeat the monologue. When you have finished, turn the lights out and leave the room. Repeat the entire workout 3 times.

Workout

62 Large circle of attention

Preparation
A walk in the park 1 (workout 17).

What to do
Imagine a small circle of attention. Breathe in and out. Imagine you are using the air from just that small circle.

Add humming to the outward breath. Repeat the exercise using the medium circle of attention. Now breathe in and out using the air from as far as you can see. Imagine the hum is filling the whole space (in truth, it is only as loud as with the medium or small circles of attention).

Duration
Switch between small, medium, and large circles for 15 minutes.

Context

No piece of acting stands alone. There is always a history supporting your character; a reason why your character is motivated to say the lines in a certain way with a specific underlying emotion attached to them.

If you think about it, the same is true in everyday life. Your life consists of a chain of events, each one having an effect on the one that comes next. It could even be said that the reason for what you are about to do is based on what you are doing now. So the same must be true of the characters you play. It is your responsibility as an actor to bring the character to life, therefore you are obliged to consider context.

Monologue 2a: male role

Jon (eating): *If she does that one more time I swear I'm going to do something about it. Last week she went through my clothes. Now she wants to go out all the time. I don't know what to do. What could possibly be next? Janice and I are both worried sick.*

Read the play carefully.

Why bother to read the play and discover the context of the scene?

Context should never be taken for granted. It is easy to misinterpret and misjudging it can seriously throw your whole interpretation off-balance. For example, monologues 2a and 2b (from both the male and female points of view) seems to be about a parent worried about his or her daughter. Yet how do you know, for example, that this isn't a comic piece in which the characters are fretting over a new puppy?

Your characterizations are likely to be shallow if you don't understand them fully. If you don't study the context of the piece, it is likely that your character will become clichéd and two-dimensional. Stanislavski believed there had to be a reason behind each word spoken and every movement made.

Monologue 2b: female role

Janice (eating): *If she does that one more time I swear I'm going to do something about it. Last week she took my clothes. Now she wants to go out all the time. I don't know what to do. What could possibly be next? Jon and I are both worried sick.*

Tip: Context
The chances of an audition panel being familiar with the play from which you pick your monologue are very high. Remember that they see hundreds of pieces every week. So study the context of the play thoroughly.

Be a detective

Finding out "why" a character says or does something provides clues as to how you might play the character more realistically. The options are endless, so always read the entire play to glean all the information you need. Then put on your detective's hat and start asking all the right questions. Here are some questions you could ask yourself about either Janice's or Jon's character in monologues 2a and 2b on pages 66 and 67.

The "who":
- Who is Jon?
- What job does he do?
- Who is Jon talking to? Is it someone he loves and trusts or someone who has had an affair with his wife? How would this affect your interpretation of the role?

The "what":
- What has just happened to your character in the moments before the monologue scene begins? Asking this kind of question will give you excellent clues as to the character's emotional state and why they act like they do.

The "when":
- What day/ month/ year is it?
- How old is Jon?

The "where":
- Where is Jon now?
- Where does he live? Work?
- Where does he want to go? Where does he aspire to be next year/ in five years/ ten years?

The "why":
- Why are they so upset?
- Do they have another child who did the same thing and suffered?
- Do they have another child who is totally different?
- Is this their first child and are they therefore feeling inadequate about dealing with the situation?
- Is there a mental disease in their family backgrounds and are they worried that it has been passed on to their daughter?
- Do they feel that their daughter might be planning to run away?
- Does either of the parents secretly want her to?
- Do they feel guilty because of something they may have said or done to the daughter?

Establishing context

Before you go to your audition, it's crucial to establish the social and historical setting of the piece. Work with the information given in the play, then use your imagination to add depth to the character, and bring the scene to life.

Social context

Where does the scene unfold? In what town? In what country? To what social class do Janice/Jon belong? Are they rich, poor, or somewhere in between? The piece would be performed in a radically different manner if Janice was a highly paid attorney talking calmly and privately to her psychiatrist than if she was a drunken factory worker talking to her best friend in their local downtown bar.

Historical context

The historical setting of the piece will affect the way in which the lines are performed. For example, if Jon were a 1960s hippie he would express himself very differently than if he were a punk in 1979.

Stanislavski and the use of "imagination"

Stanislavki called what you could find in the text the **given circumstances**. However, he also saw the need to enliven your characterization. In other words, you often have to go beyond the text and begin to use your imagination to fill in the gaps. If things are not explained in the play then you need to invent them based on the information you do have. By doing this you will develop a fuller **character history**.

Workout

63 **Character history**

Preparation

Pen and paper.

Invent a full character history for either Jon or Janice (monologues 2a and 2b, pages 66 and 67) by answering the questions below:

- How old is your character?
- Where do they work?
- What's their favorite color?
- Who are they talking to?

Add 10 more basic questions of your own.

Now develop the context by imagining that your character has a secret:

What?— What is the secret?
Why?— Why do they have secret?
Who?— Who is involved in the secret? In what way?
How?— How does this affect how your character acts?

What to do

Perform the monologue based on the invented context.

Duration

Repeat a number of times until the performance is fluid. Now repeat the entire exercise developing a different character history.

Tip: Don't over-think it
Studying context is meant to help not hinder your performance. Once you have done your homework make sure that you do not think too much as you perform. Simply do the work and set the character free. If you over-think as you are acting the impression you give does not seem "alive" or "spontaneous."

Interpreting historical and social context

Here is an example of some basic research about the Russian aristocracy around the turn of the 1900s and how it could be interpreted:

1. **Most of the men would have been in the army.**
2. **The women wore corsets.**
3. **Many of the aristocracy lived in big houses in the countryside, miles from anywhere.**

1. The fact that most men would have served in the army gives us clues about movement and voice. When playing a young man of this time you are likely to stand very upright, walk very definitely, and perhaps, because you would have been a general, have a condescending air to those you feel are "beneath" you. For example, you may turn away from those you do not respect or invade their personal space. You might even use a dismissive tone of voice.

2. The fact that the women wore corsets gives you clues as to their emotional state. Naturally a corset would greatly affect all of your movement. There would also be a huge amount of physical pressure on your ribs, making it hard to breathe, and this together with a social code about how women should look and behave suggests that you are physically and emotionally repressed. Conversely, the corset would physically pull your shape into a "perfect" figure and you would be seen as beautiful and desirable.

3. The fact that you lived miles from anywhere means that visitors would be rare. This creates a high level of boredom and tension between the people in the house. If there is someone in the house who you do not like, then the tension is heightened, as are all of the relationships. Therefore you may act outside of the social code, causing a conflict within your character who is trying to behave as he or she should. If you are an unmarried woman or man, a rare visit to the house from someone of the opposite sex may cause you to act irrationally and mistake any feeling of attraction for love.

A rigid military-type posture, with hands clasped behind the back, would be a characteristic of an army officer.

Workout

64 Historical and social influences

Preparation
Here is another historical/social fact about the Russian upper classes of the time:
• Even for the aristocracy, money could easily run out leaving them broke with an image to maintain.

What to do
Add this extra fact to what you already know (above).
Imagine that a rich landowner is coming to visit your house.
As an actor how might this effect your movement and voice?
Write down your ideas.

Tip: Do your research
Research the playwright for clues as to how to perform the play. For example, Anton Chekhov—who wrote about Russia at this time—wanted his audience to see how ridiculous the behavior of the upper classes had become. In other words, what seems like a very serious play on the page needs to have a comic undertone to achieve its goal.

Program 4: week 4

Replace Program 3 with Program 4. You will continue to carry out many basic exercises in Program 4 because it is important to gather as much strength as possible in these foundation areas.

Morning Session (50 minutes)

Workout 1
Basic lying down.

What to do:
Lie down in the basic lying down position.
Duration:
5 minutes.
Aim:
Release tension in the body.
Add workout 50 for 10 minutes.

Workouts 4 and 5
Baby in a buggy/ Rolling baby.

What to do:
Baby in a buggy coming up into Rolling baby.
Duration:
Baby in a buggy for 3 minutes.
Rolling baby: 5 repetitions each way.
Aim:
Increase flexibility and strength.

Workouts 34 and 35
Adding sound to the breath.

Duration:
Do 10 repetitions of each workout. Take a short break in between but continue to lie down in the basic lying down position.

Aim:
Strengthen the breathing and connect the sound to the breath.

Workout 10
Preparation for neutral walking 2.

Duration:
Repeat the exercise 5 times. Then take a break before repeating.
Aim:
Continue to strengthen basic posture.

Workouts 37 and 38
Resonating the voice.

Duration:
Repeat each workout on 5 breaths.
Aim:
Increase vocal resonance.

Everyday life

Workout 17
Walk in the park 1.
Go for a walk in the park twice a week to get the body used to neutral positioning.

Workouts 39
Walk in the park 3.
Do this for 15 minutes, twice a week. This will strengthen your vocal resonance.

Workouts 23–26
Observational workouts.
Pick one workout from 23–26, twice a week. These observational exercises will help you become aware of tension in yourself and others.

Weekly

Aim:
To practice contextualizing a character.

What to do:
Read at least one play per week. Choose a character. Research the time period and place. Look at what the text reveals about your character. Use your imagination to bring the character to life.

Evening Session (45 minutes)

Workout 3
Advanced lying down.

What to do:
Lie down in the basic lying down position.
Duration:
10 minutes (instead of 5) of lying down before starting the movement.
Aim:
Release the tension of the day before working on strengthening the back.

Workouts 5 and 6
Rolling baby/Baby trying to crawl.

Duration:
5 slow repetitions of Rolling baby coming up into 3 minutes of Baby trying to crawl.
Aim:
Increase flexibility and strength.

Workout 8
Rolling down the wall.

What to do:
Gently roll up and down one vertebra at a time.
Duration:
3 slow repetitions of Rolling down the wall.
Aim:
Balance and align the spine while standing up. Rolling down the wall (3 slow repetitions).

Workouts 9–17
Neutral movement.

What to do:
Choose any three of these exercises.
Duration:
Every day (Monday to Friday).
Aim:
Continue to educate the body in neutral movement.

Workouts 33
Spontaneous breathing 2.

What to do:
Extinguish the three candles in sequence.
Duration:
Repeat 5 times. Rest in between.
Aim:
Strengthen the diaphragm.

Workout 43
Connecting the vowel sounds to the hum 2.

Duration:
Repeat 5 times as workout states.
Aim:
Connect the vowel sounds to the breath.

Workout 44
Connecting consonant sounds to vowel sounds.

What to do:
Run through the workout using the sounds specified.
Duration:
1 repetition.
Aim:
Increase flexibility and strength.

Workouts 48 and 49
Energizing the mouth.

What to do:
Repeat each tongue twister with your finger in your mouth, then repeat each tongue twister holding your tongue, then repeat each simply speaking normally.
Duration:
Repeat the above sequence twice.
Aim:
To energize and free the mouth.

Mini Program 4
Morning session (15 minutes)

Workout 1
Lie in the basic position for 5 minutes.

Workout 3
Repeat this workout for 10 minutes.

Everyday life (15 minutes)

Workout 17
Walk in the park once a week.

Workout 39
Walk in the park 3.
Walk in the park for 15 minutes, twice a week.

Workouts 23–26
Observational workouts.
Choose one workout from 23–26. Twice a week.

Evening session (15 minutes)

Workouts 45–47
Repeat each tongue twister with your finger in your mouth. Repeat each tongue twister holding your tongue. Repeat each tongue twister speaking normally.

Becoming a character in a play is all about knowing the individual you are playing inside and out. Whether you are a lonely teenager looking for love, a 23rd-century astronaut fighting aliens, or a modern-day cannibal hungry for his dinner, you need to understand your character. You do this by finding a set of reasons to explain why they behave as they do.

Chapter 5: Character

The next level

As an actor, knowing your character well inspires a sense of freedom and the confidence to be playful and spontaneous with your interpretation. Then, once you understand your character's motivation (why they do what they do), you will develop more of an understanding on an emotional level. You can then develop a feeling of empathy with the person you are creating.

Loving your character

Many first-rate actors go so far as saying that in order to play a character convincingly you have to "love" that individual as you would a brother or a sister. If you find the good in them then the audience will do so too, and your performance will be seen as rounded and well developed. Research is vital but it is the feeling of personal connection and liberation that ultimately brings a character to life.

Tip: Physicalization

Physicalization is a way of moving from the "mental" process to the "feeling" process. Basically, you form the body language of your character from your research. Then, after you have "physicalized" your ideas in this way, you encourage the character's emotion to emerge as if it were your own.

From context to reality

Once you have studied the context, used your imagination, and constructed your character history, you are ready to "experiment" with your character's emotional and mental state. There are two main areas to consider: these are internal and external. The internal represents your character's thoughts and their emotional state. The external relates to how your character shows these states to the other characters and to the audience.

How to internalize your character history

To "know" your character's internal emotional state by studying the play, and to "feel" your character's emotions as if they were your own, are two very different things. In fact, they can sometimes seem so far apart that the mental "knowing" actually blocks the genuine emotion altogether. They must be brought together and this chapter will show you how.

Tip: Do it larger than life
When developing a character, it is a good idea to exaggerate any body language that is involved. This larger-than-life approach allows you to clarify movements and gestures and to connect with them fully. Do not, however, overplay the gestures in your performance unless the style of the piece specifically demands it.

Workout

 Social status

Preparation
Imagine that your character comes from a very wealthy, modern, social background.

What to do
Look at monologue 3 on pge 79. Character observation. Observe people of this type socializing. Notice the body language. Especially notice how they stand. What position are their feet in? Are their hips slightly pushed forward, backward, or are they central? How do they hold their back and neck? Do they hold their head high? Do they tend to look downward or upward? Observe their gestures, for example, the position of their arms and use of their hands.

The script says that the character is drinking, so observe them drinking. What is their favorite drink? How do they hold the glass? How do they place the glass down after they have had a sip and do they relinquish the glass or keep it in their hand until they bring it to their mouth again? How eagerly do they perform this action?

Duration
15 minutes.

Tip: Remember the rules about observation
Don't be obvious or judgmental when involved in observation exercises. Your subjects are helping you. Remember that in order to play a character effectively you have to understand him or her at a deeper level, and genuinely feel affection and a connection to them.

Workout

 Taking on a different body language

Preparation
Put on a pair of shoes that are similar to those of your character.

What to do
Stand in the neutral position (see workout 7) wearing the shoes you have chosen. Now move your feet in a way suggested by the style of the shoes and shift your weight around so you are standing in a way that your character would stand. Now focus on the hips. Are they forward, backward, or central? Now notice the back and the neck. Allow them to find their place.

Walk around the room, vary the pace, sit down, stand, and perform various movements in the shoes. Allow your character's movement to emerge.

Duration
15 minutes.

Tip: Exaggerate
Exaggerate the movement to begin with and then gradually reduce the size of the movement so that it is more natural.

Allow your character to grow from the feet upward.

The Process

Internalizing external observations

Once you have done your observations of your character consider the following two questions:

• In what part(s) of the body does your character hold blocks?

For example, if they sit and work at a computer all day, their eyes might be strained such that they no longer see very clearly. (This could be described as having "blocked" vision.) They might hold tension in their lower back and shoulders causing "blocks" in other parts of the body. If they have any sexual issues then tension might be held in the hips and lower stomach areas.

• In what part(s) of the body is your character particularly relaxed and where does the movement seem freer?

Perhaps there is a free flow of movement in the arms and the hands of your character, or perhaps their back seems to expand widely and be supple, or perhaps their movement of the head is articulate and flexible. Watching dancers, athletes, or children will give you a good sense of how the body moves when energy and the breath flow freely through it.

How to interpret physical blocks

After this exploration you need to incorporate your physical observations into your own body. To begin with, practice the blocks as imagined pain or held tension in that particular area of the body and then imagine the source of the physical block. For example, if your character has eye strain then imagine you have a constant headache. See what this does to your body language. If their hips are tense, imagine that you have a constant pain in your hips when walking as the result of an injury.

If your hands are clenched, then imagine that you are angry at a colleague at work. This, however, is only the beginning. Once the body language is integrated in your body, then practice the movement so that it becomes more comfortable and more natural both to you and to those observing you.

Tip
You need to observe the subject's vocal patterns, range, and tones. While maintaining as free a voice as possible, try and experience the vocal habits that you observe. If you are aware of tension in their voice, perhaps a hardening of tone, then find a similar expression in your voice for short periods of time. It is important to return to your own freer voice so that you do not damage your vocal apparatus.

Monologue 3
(The character is drinking)

"I sometimes get very aggressive when I've had a drink. Only sometimes. At other times I become a different sort of person altogether." (Pause) "Some people say that I am unpredictable. Sam used to tell me that all the time. 'You're just too damn unpredictable' he used to say. 'I never know what you're going to do next.' But he doesn't tell me that any more. He doesn't say very much at all. I guess not knowing what you're going to do next has its advantages."

Learn this monologue by heart.

67 Discovering and expressing your character's emotions

Preparation
Imagine that the character persona you adopted in workout 65 is also secretly very angry. Create a plausible scenario that would give rise to the anger. Don't forget they are very upper class and so probably would not show a huge amount of emotion externally. They would be very controlled, with evidence of anger in their body language. Internally there might be a great deal of held tension in the body, but perhaps some of the external gestures are freer in order to camouflage the anger.
Connect to the body language and gestures you have found to express this emotion.

What to do
Once you have taken on the adapted body language, perform monologue 3 (below).

Duration
Repeat 3 or 4 times, each time discovering something about the character through the monologue. Allow your instincts and impulses to guide and free expression as you speak the monologue. Begin with exaggerated body language and gradually allow the movement to become more natural.

Run consecutively through the emotions your character experiences in the monologue, trying to naturally feel the transitions between each emotion.

Keeping your acting alive

Stanislavski observed that moments that have passed in real life cannot be brought back in exactly the same way they were initially experienced. If you try to recreate them, they will inevitably change. This has a parallel in performance. If during a performance you start trying to repeat exactly what you did the night before, then your acting will not be spontaneous. It is expected that your movement will stay similar and the same goes for the delivery of your lines. However, you should not try to repeat your best performance; instead develop a new one every time.

Workout

 68 Social status— a different context

Preparation
Imagine your character is from a blue-collar social background.

What to do
Character observation: go out. Observe people from a blue-collar background. Notice the body language, especially how they stand.

• What position are their legs and feet in?
• Are their hips slightly pushed forward, backward, or are they central?
• How do they hold their back and neck?
• Do they hold their head high?
• Do they tend to look downward or upward?

Observe their gestures. Observe them eating. Return home and assume a similar body language.

Duration
Observe for up to 1 hour. Body language: 30 minutes.

Workout

 69 From physical to emotional

Preparation
Now imagine that the character in workout 68 is extremely upset (sad, not angry). Physically take on this character's body language and then allow it to collapse in on itself as if someone has dealt a blow to your stomach. Create a reason for this state.

What to do
Once you have taken on the body language, perform monologue 3 (page 79). Allow the emotion to emerge a little more with each repetition. Conversely, as the emotion gets stronger, with each performance make the body language smaller so that it is more natural. Don't think about facial expressions. If anything, allow the muscles of the face to be relaxed so that the emotion will naturally and realistically mold the expression.

Duration
Repeat 4 or 5 times. Rest and repeat the monologue twice.

Workout

70 Adding character to neutral standing 1

Workout position Neutral standing (workout 7).

What to do
Answer this question:
Which of these two category descriptions best describes your character?
• Thinker
• Works with their hands

Thinker:
If your character is more of a thinker, then slightly lift the chin so the face is toward the ceiling.
    Now, from the feet upward, give everything a slight lift.

Worker:
If your character is a worker or craftsman, tilt the chin downward and relax the knees, bringing the character closer to the earth.

Layering
Layering means gradually adding more and more levels to your character. For example, in workout 68 the basic layer was that the character was of a blue-collar background. On top of this you added another layer of emotional upset. On this page are two more examples of physical layering.

What you want
For the position to seem real.

What you don't want
To strain the neck by sticking the chin forward.

Lean forward.

Workout

71 Adding character to neutral standing 2

Workout position
Neutral standing (workout 7).

What to do
Answer this question:
Which of these two descriptions best describes your character?
• Looking toward the future
• Thinking about (or trapped by) the past

If your character is mostly thinking about what he or she is going to do then lean forward slightly. Move your weight slightly onto the balls of your feet.
    If your character is mostly thinking about the past then put the weight slightly more onto the heels. The stance is upright. Don't give your character a backward lean. Keep your character's movements subtle.
    Now you've got the basis of forward, backward, and up and down, you can begin to introduce more detailed work.

Put weight on the balls of your feet.

Advanced exercises

Stanislavski says that to fully understand a character you need to practice playing that person in different situations outside of the text. Most people spend most of their lives doing mundane things, so to understand our character we need to experience them in these types of ordinary situations.

Workout

72 Deepening character 1

Preparation
Decide on a modern-day character of your own. Create a social background. Create a character history. Find your character's body language.

What to do
Have your character perform everyday tasks in the house. Tidy your room. Cook the dinner. Watch the TV. Remember you perform these tasks as if you are in that situation. This does not mean that you totally become the character. You play the character as if you are in that situation, always maintaining a sense of awareness that you are acting.

Duration
15 minutes maximum.

Help!
If I'm playing an angry character then how can I do workout 73?
• This workout is about finding your character by doing routine and mundane tasks. Simply play your character on one of their "good days"; plan a scenario for them.

Workout

73 Deepening character 2

Preparation
Remind yourself of the character you developed in workout 72.

What to do
This time go outside. Make sure you go to a place where you are not known, but not anywhere where playing your character would put you in an awkward or vulnerable situation. In public places, play your character but tone down the character's most extreme emotions. It is a question of degree. The more passionate expression of these emotions can be explored with a friend, in your bedroom in front of the mirror, or with your director if the play requires this of the character.

Duration
15 minutes.

Staying in control
To play the character as if you are in that situation means that you are being very realistic both internally and externally, but there is always a sense of you knowing that you are not that character. To become the person completely is not acting. To immerse yourself totally in the character, so that there is no longer a sense of distance between you and the character, may be unhelpful because you might no longer have a sense of control or play. Also, on the stage you may not be able to follow stage directions or respond to various technical cues. In film you may not be able to follow the director's careful advice. This self-control is your safety net and you must never work without it.

With this careful control you can more readily release yourself from the character you have built and assume your own natural body and self after the performance is over. When actors become the person they are playing, without awareness, the performances are often self-indulgent, introverted, and ineffective.

Tip: Don't over-embellish
Don't bring anything to the role that isn't needed. Don't layer in any cleverly added extras.

Sharing your performance

Now you know how to do your research and then transfer it onto and into yourself. What you are striving for is to seem naturalistic but at the same time to have an awareness of what you are doing. Also you must get the audience to empathize with your character and you know to do this by understanding the character and connecting with them yourself.

The mistake many inexperienced actors make is to stop at this point. But, what is the use of developing and internalizing a character if you don't share him or her externally with your audience?

> **Help!**
> I still don't understand how to do it!
> • When you are working with a small circle of attention it is as if you are drawing the attention of the audience toward you, thereby creating an intimacy between you and the audience. You act like a magnet. A good exercise is to simply imagine this when you are performing. When working with the larger circles imagine yourself literally filling the room.

Workout

74   Sharing your performance

Preparation
Remind yourself about circles of attention in workouts 58–62.

What to do
Perform monologue 3 (page 79). Imagine that your character is a controlled and calculating murderer. Find time to invent a history and understand their motivation. Perform in character using a small circle of attention.

Duration
2 repetitions. Now repeat the workout using medium and large circles of attention.

Small   Medium   Large

Finding your character's voice

Many actors find that if they capture the voice of their character then everything else seems to fall into place. There are six technical elements for you to consider when discovering your character's vocal expression.

 ## Register

This means how high or low your character speaks, or the pitch of the voice. Often an exaggerated register, one that is outside your natural range of expression, can be used to develop a more comic character. However, in naturalistic situations it is often best to use your natural vocal range because this is more readily linked to your natural emotions. So any adaptations in register are usually slight and subtle.

 ## Placement

Where in the body does your character place (and therefore resonate) their voice? For example, for comic effect the voice may be placed in the nose, or perhaps it might be very breathy to denote a lady who is stereotypically sexy. For drama, the voice is placed in its natural center.

 ## Inflection

This is the natural rise and fall of the voice during speech. For example, when you ask a question the voice rises at the end of the sentence, so causing an upward inflection. If you make a firm or declarative statement then it tends to fall. Most inflections are subtle and natural and are determined by the thoughts, feelings, and intentions of the character you are playing.

 ## Pacing

Pacing is the speed at which your character speaks. This also includes slowing down, speeding up, and pausing. The pacing during your performance depends mostly on the kind of play you are performing and your character's intentions and emotional state. For example the line, "Oh my God, he's dead" would be spoken very differently by a character in a comic situation who has just accidentally shot her husband, to a woman in a drama who's been living at the bedside of her dying child for months.

Tip: Pacing your character
Stanislavski believed that characters should have their own unique pace. He meant the general speed and level of energy at which they go about living their lives and performing their tasks on the stage. This speed is totally unique to the character, and therefore it makes him or her stand out as an individual. It also contrasts them to all the other characters in the play.

 ## Emphasis

This is the stress that is put onto certain words to clarify the meaning. There are three ways of emphasizing:

a. Pausing

If you pause before a word it will keep the audience waiting, and therefore place importance on that word in their minds. If you pause after a word this will give the audience slightly more time to think about the meaning and therefore give it emphasis. For example, "I think the (pause) murderer is Jeremy!" or "I think the murderer is (pause) Jeremy!" Pauses are also a way to create dramatic tension (see page 104 for more on pausing).

b. Stressing

You can choose to stress the word itself to emphasize the parts of the phrase that you want to draw attention to: "I can't believe you **killed** him" or "I can't believe **you** killed him" or "I can't believe you killed **him**." In each of these cases either the action of killing, the killer, or the victim is emphasized.

c. Emotional emphasis

This is very subtle and happens when you invest a particular word (or phrase) with more emotion than the rest. The effect of this is to reveal a character's internal life and to give the audience information on what is important to the speaker.

 ## Accent and dialect

Accent is normally used to describe the vocal patterns of somebody from a distinct country. For example, an American accent or an English accent would identify the country of origin of the speaker. Dialect denotes whereabouts in that country they are from. For example, America (accent), New York (dialect). Cities like New York also contain very distinct and varying dialects within them, so America (accent), New York (dialect), Bronx (dialect). Or England (accent), London (dialect), East End (dialect).

Playing comedic characters

The basic techniques of playing comedy effectively are often very misunderstood. It is assumed that you have to play the character in a "funny way" to achieve a successful performance but the fact is that the exact opposite is true. More often than not, to do comedy well you have to play the character with exaggerated seriousness, sincerity, and earnestness. It is this which brings the comedy about. For example, if your character is obsessively concerned about the neatness of their appearance, then it is all the more funny when they fall headlong into a pile of horse manure.

If you are just trying to make your character funny, comic situations won't be so effective and your acting will not be seen as intelligently played. Remember that a character in a comedy does not know they are playing in a comedy but you, the actor, do.

Don't go for laughs from the characterization alone. If you concentrate on the exaggerated reality, the pacing, and the timing, the laughter will spontaneously arise. Release yourself from the pressure of "getting a laugh" and it will give your work an added sense of freedom. It is more important that the audience enjoys your performance as a whole, and feels empathy for your character than laughs out loud at one or two funny moments. If you take clowning as a classic example, you will see that the most effective clowns are not those who simply rely on a clever slapstick routine and a pie in the face. A good clown will develop personality and character so that the audience can relate to them and their situation; then they take the hit. A tit-for-tat story of revenge can then emerge with pies getting bigger and bigger and the audience will be fully engaged for the ride.

Even if your character is ridiculously silly, the audience needs to believe that he or she has the qualities of a real person. Only then will the audience connect with them. They need to know that your character can feel joy and sadness within their silliness. Always keep your character up-beat and with a drive that comes from the knowledge that everything will be alright in the end. In comedy it really is essential to love the character you're playing—and to allow yourself to enjoy playing them.

Workout

75 Experimenting with register

Preparation
Read monologue 4 (opposite).

What to do
Experiment first with the character's register while reading the text aloud. Don't be afraid of going totally over the top here. Keep yourself relaxed and free. Remember we are just finding a starting point here.

Duration
Try three or four different registers ranging from low to high. Which feels right?

Workout

76 Adding vocal placement

Preparation
Remind yourself of workout 75.

What to do
Now add vocal placement to monologue 4 (opposite). You will see that this is a cold environment.

First place the voice in the nose and read the text aloud. Now repeat the exercise with a breathy voice in the mouth (again expressing the cold). Remember to keep the whole thing exaggerated. Which felt better? Maybe you have an idea of your own to try?

Duration
Repeat as necessary until you arrive at a choice that feels right.

Monologue 4

Two supermarket workers find themselves trapped in the meat refrigeration unit.

"This is an extremely unusual situation. I mean, who'd have thought, me and you, in an icebox? What a coincidence eh? Who'd have thought eh? Who'd have thought it? Well. No one probably. No one I know anyway. Not that I know many people. I don't...So... Me and you. Trapped. Together. Trapped for eternity. In an icebox. Frozen. Frozen like two Popsicles on sticks. It's not like it was planned or anything. Well maybe by God. Just not planned by me. Well he does move in mysterious ways. God I mean. My cousin Jean says that God's a load of rubbish but I beg to differ. Still, it takes all sorts to make a world. So. So. Erm. best make the most of it eh? It's freezing. Maybe we should huddle up for warmth. Maybe not."

Tip
Some actors find that by reading the text aloud a few times the voice and personality of the character emerge by themselves. Follow your instinct and don't second guess yourself when you want to try different ways of speaking the text.

Workout

Pacing your work

Preparation
Remind yourself of workouts 75 and 76.

What to do
Read monologue 4 aloud (above). This time experiment with the pacing. See what you feel is the natural rhythm of the piece and then allow it to be exaggerated. Once you have achieved this add emphasis to certain words and see how this alters the meaning.

Duration
Repeat as necessary. What kind of choices emerge?

Playing dramatic characters

Acting a dramatic role certainly has its challenges. Stanislavski talks about the need for emotional truth, therefore giving depth to a performance. But how do you find the emotional truth? Stanislavski puts it quite plainly: "Truth on the stage is whatever we can believe in sincerely."

When he was first developing his acting method, Stanislavski believed in emotional memory. This was the actor's ability to recall their "most absorbing memories" from the past and to connect to them again when necessary. For example, if your character is grieving over the death of a loved one then you might remember a similar time in your own life and recall the emotion.

The biggest danger of this type of work is that there is a tendency for the actor to become too self-absorbed and so less inclined to share their emotion openly with the audience. There can also be a tendency to force feelings too directly, pushing an old emotion forth rather than creating it anew and rediscovering it more spontaneously each time it is performed.

Modern-day actors now know that to have actual experience of the event you are playing is not necessary. They trust to observation, imagination, and an ability to "tune in" to a character. Ideally, the modern-day actor needs to be sensitive, open, and able to play their emotions like a musical instrument. Only then does "tuning in" become possible. In the end, you will discover which method, or combination of methods is most effective for you as an actor.

Tip: how to approach this style
When approaching the dramatic script, work the opposite way to comedy. Start quietly and work up.

Workout

78 Learning from the professionals 1

Preparation
Rent a serious movie or go and see a dramatic play.

What to do
Study the register, pacing, placement, inflection, and emphasis used by one of the main actors. Learn a section of the dialogue and perform it in your own way. Always remember to experiment and be playful.

Workout

79 Learning from the professionals 2

Preparation
Rent a comic movie or go and see a comedy on the stage.

What to do
Study the difference in register, pacing, placement, inflection, and emphasis used by one of the main characters when compared to the drama in workout 78—if possible, watch the same actor as in the comedy. Learn a section of the dialogue and perform it in your own way.

Tip
It is fine to learn from other actors but never imitate them. You must be yourself and discover your own choices.

Monologue 5: In a restaurant.

"I will not keep quiet about this. I will not keep quiet. I have kept quiet my entire life. I will not keep my voice down now. All right. And once, just for once I'm not going to care. All right! Did you get that? Did you get that? I don't give a damn.

Listen. Listen to me properly. Jonny. Listen properly, just for once. Now. Now I'm telling. Now at 27 years old I'm telling: I gave people what they wanted. Jonny, I gave people what they wanted every single dirty day and all of those dirty nights. I did what I was meant to. I gave people what they wanted, whatever they asked for. Night after night. And when I did that, even when I did that, nobody, nobody gave me anything back. Why does nobody ever give anything back? Jonny?"

Workout

80 Working quietly to find the emotion

Preparation
Familiarize yourself with the dramatic monologue above.

What to do
Read it aloud, extremely quietly and slowly, even repeating words or phrases if you are so inclined. Notice how when you do this, the emotional content arises much more easily. To achieve a credible character, keep the register and placement close to your own natural voice.

Duration
Repeat 2 or 3 more times, allowing it to be different each time. Give yourself time to reflect on the discoveries that you are making. After this, still keeping it quiet, start experimenting with emphasis.

Playing a serio-comedic character

Although pure comedy can contain some social criticism, serio-comedy often contains it in abundance. It is aimed at exposing society in what can seem like an abrupt and cruel way in order to convey the writer's point of view. *One Flew Over the Cuckoo's Nest* is a wonderful example of a film in this style and *A Day in the Death of Joe Egg* by Peter Nichols is a great example of a serio-comic play.

This serio-comedic style certainly is popular with audiences and actors alike. However, it has been likened to playing with fire, as one slip-up in the acting can turn a dangerously funny comedy into a hugely insulting, offensive piece of theater. Playing this type of character needs to be handled with great care.

Serio-comedy should never be played for individual laughs. The situation should only be laugh-out-loud funny when those dreadfully biased words tumble out of your character's mouth with total sincerity. Your character needs to believe totally that their point of view is absolutely the only one. The God-given truth. Characters in these sorts of plays tend to have an incredibly restricted view of life and little understanding of the feelings of others.

Not surprisingly, serio-comedy is acted somewhere between the dramatic and comic styles. This does not mean that the piece swings from one style to the other, rather that you create a new style that is situated in between that of drama and comedy.

The monologue on this page is a piece of serio-comedy. This simple-minded young character has been locked in the bathroom. All the audience sees is the bathroom door. Lulu is a cat, and Julia is a friend who the character thinks is in the room but actually is not. (When the playwright uses the word "beat" he means "pause.")

Monologue 6
[Shouting from the bathroom]

"Forty-nine minutes [Beat] Forty-damn-nine-damn-minutes [Beat] Where's Lulu? Where's Lulu? [Calls] Julia. Where's Lulu? [Calling] Lulu. Lulu [Beat] I know what you're like. I said—I know what you're like. You better not've lost her. LULU! [Beat] Where's my shoes? Julia. Where's my shoes? [Beat] Very nice. Thank you. I said very nice thank you. Thanks for trying. You're so damn welcome. [Beat] LULU! [Beat] Oh that's all-shitty-all right then [Beat. Calling for the cat] Lulu. Lulu. LULU! [As if he/she has banged themselves] Ow! Crap. What the hell [Beat] Where are my damn socks? [Beat] Julia? Julia? [Beat] Julia. [Beat] Where is she? Where is she? Julia's invisible. Oh where's Julia? Oh nice. Oh she's not here. Where's Julia? Oh. I don't know. Could be anywhere. [Beat] I'm still looking for my socks in Timbuktu. Julia. Julia? You'd better not be dead or it won't be funny."

Workout

 81 Developing a serio-comic character 1

Preparation
Study monologue 6 (opposite).

What to do
Now read the monologue aloud, extremely quietly and slowly. Focus on allowing the emotional content to arise.

Duration
Repeat as necessary. Move directly onto workout 82.

Workout

82 Developing a serio-comic character 2

Preparation
Do workout 81.

What to do
Read the monologue aloud. Allow the character to be exaggerated. Develop register and placement. Experiment with pacing and timing.

Duration
Repeat 2 or 3 times, allowing it to be different each time. After this start experimenting with emphasis. Wait 5 minutes to reflect on what you have discovered and then perform the monologue. Having approached it from both a dramatic (workout 80) and comic (workout 81) angle, you should have the beginnings of a serio-comic style.

Tip
Don't be afraid to ignore written pauses or to add some of your own.

Program 5: week 5

It's time to replace Program 4 with Program 5. You will continue to carry out many basic exercises in Program 5, because it is important to gather as much strength as possible in these foundation areas. If you have limited time, then follow the Mini Program.

Morning Session (55 minutes)

Workout 1
Basic lying down.

What to do:
Lie down in the basic lying down position.
Duration:
5 minutes.
Aim:
Release the tension in the body.

Workouts 4 and 5
Baby in a buggy/
Rolling baby.

What to do:
Baby in a buggy coming up into Rolling baby.
Duration:
Baby in a buggy for 3 minutes.
Rolling baby: 5 repetitions each way.
Aim:
Increase flexibility and strength.

Workouts 34 and 35
Adding sound to the breath.

Duration:
Do 10 repetitions of each workout. Take a break in between but continue to lie in basic lying down position.
Aim:
Strengthen the breathing and connect the sound to the breath.

Workout 10
Preparation for neutral walking 2.

Duration:
Repeat the exercise 5 times. Then take a break before repeating again.
Aim:
Continue to strengthen basic posture.

Workouts 37 and 38
Resonating the voice.

Duration:
Repeat each workout on 5 breaths.
Aim:
Increase vocal resonance.

Weekly

Aim:
To practice contextualizing a character.

What to do:
Read at least one play per week. Choose a character. Research the time period and place. Look at what the text reveals about your character. Use your imagination to bring the character to life.

Everyday life

Workout 17
Walk in the park 1.
Go for a walk in the park twice a week to get the body used to neutral positioning.

Workout 39
Walk in the park 3.
Do this workout for 15 minutes, twice a week. This will strengthen your vocal resonance.

Workouts 23–26
Observational workouts.
Choose one workout from 23–26, twice a week. These observational exercises will help you to become aware of tension in both yourself and others.

Evening Session (45 minutes)

Workout 3
Advanced lying down.

What to do:
Lie down in the basic lying down position.
Duration:
10 minutes (instead of 5) of lying down before starting the movement.
Aim:
Release the tension of the day before working on strengthening the back.

Workouts 5 and 6
Rolling baby/Baby trying to crawl.

Duration:
5 slow repetitions of Rolling baby coming into 3 minutes of Baby trying to crawl.
Aim:
Increase flexibility and strength.

Workout 8
Rolling down the wall.

What to do:
Gently roll up and down one vertebra at a time.
Duration:
3 slow repetitions.
Aim:
Balance and align the spine while standing.

Workout 33
Spontaneous breathing 2.

What to do:
Extinguish the three candles in sequence.
Duration:
Repeat 5 times. Rest in between.
Aim:
Strengthen the diaphragm.

Workout 43
Connecting the vowel sounds to the hum 2.

Duration:
Repeat 5 times as workout states.
Aim:
Connect the vowel sounds to the breath.

Workout 44
Connecting consonant sounds to vowel sounds.

What to do:
Run through the workout using the sounds specified.
Duration:
1 repetition.
Aim:
Strengthen the consonant sounds.

Workouts 48 and 49
Energizing the mouth.

What to do:
Repeat each tongue twister with your finger in your mouth, then repeat each tongue twister holding the tongue, then repeat simply speaking normally.
Duration:
Repeat the above sequence twice.
Aim:
Energize and free the mouth.

Mini Program 5

Morning session (15 minutes)

Workout 1
Lie down in the basic position for 5 minutes.

Workout 3
Repeat this workout for 10 minutes.

Everyday life

Workout 17
Walk in the park. Once a week.

Workout 39
Walk in the park 3. Walk in the park for 15 minutes. Twice a week.

Workouts 23-26
Observational workouts. Choose one workout from 23-26. Twice a week.

Evening session (15 minutes)

Aim:
Practice contextualizing a character.

What to do:
Read at least one play per week. Choose a character. Research the time period and place. Look at what the text reveals about your character. Use your imagination to bring the character to life.

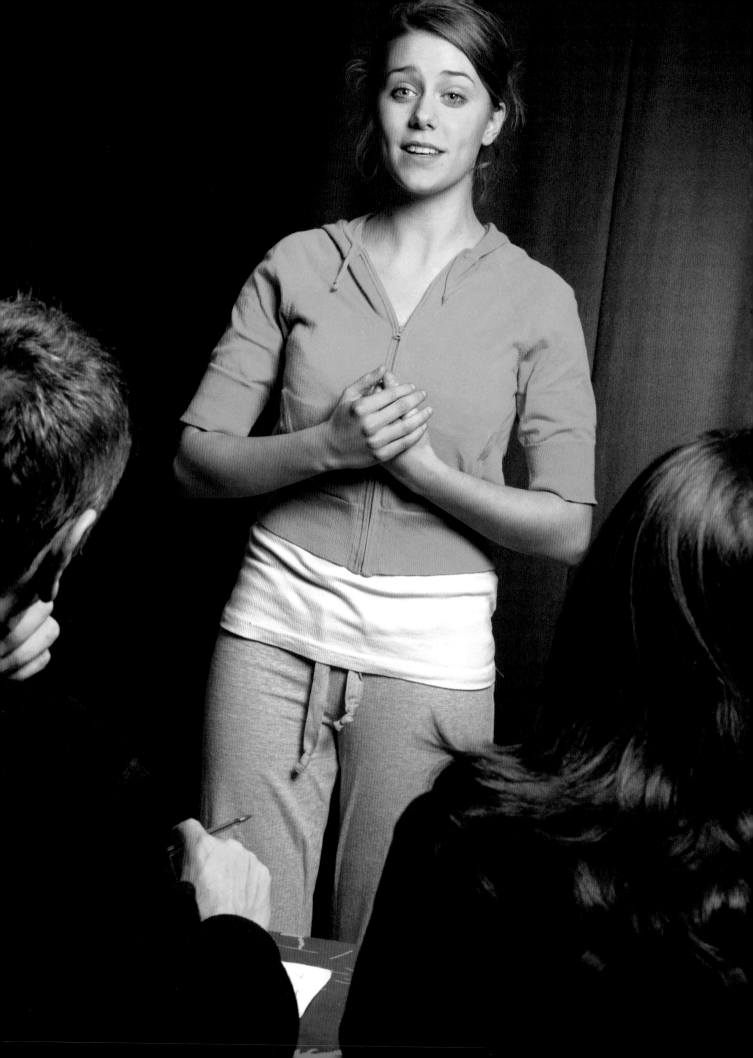

In a competitive environment such as auditions, it stands to reason that you need to be thoroughly prepared. Even if you get it right, competition is so fierce that you need to be at the very top of your game to progress to the next round. If you've done the hard graft, then you should be well on your way. Now it's time to pull everything together for the audition.

Chapter 6:
The Audition

How to prepare

The ultimate aim is to pass the audition and be accepted into the school, but there are a number of smaller goals you need to accomplish along the way to get there. The ticklist, opposite, lists the categories that are usually assessed, either consciously or subconsciously, by the panel from the moment you walk into the room (see also pages 60–61).

The best way to understand what your targets should be is to look at the process from the audition panel's point of view. Exactly what are they looking for? They may well have seen over a thousand people before you. So what will make you stand out above and beyond the rest? Use the ticklist opposite as a starting point. Become an expert at filling out theater school applications succinctly and economically, choosing your words well and telling them as much about yourself in as few words as you can. A sharp, focused writing style denotes a sharp, focused actor.

Tip
Apply to as many schools as possible. Don't limit yourself. Use the first two auditions to get used to the situation. After that go for your top choice.

Ticklist

❑ **What you look like** . . . .

. . . .

. . . .

This includes your general vibrancy and vitality (see pages 10–11), and how you are dressed (see workouts 97–98).

❑ **What you sound like** . . . .

. . . .

. . . .

The freedom of your vocal expression (see workouts 27–51).

❑ **How you move** . . . .

. . . .

. . . .

Is your movement free or restricted? (See workouts 9–26.)

❑ **Can you act?** . . . .

. . . .

Your acting ability. Can your emotion be genuinely and openly shared with the audience? Is your movement, voice, and emotion integrated? Are you able to freely express the thought and actions of the character? (See pages 75–91.)

❑ **Are you engaging?** . . . .

. . . .

. . . .

Do you hold the audience's attention throughout? (See workouts 52–56 and workout 74).

❑ **Do you understand the importance of context?** . . . .

. . . .

. . . .

Historical and social research. Are you aware of the character's development within the play? (See pages 66–71 and workouts 92–95).

Tip: The audition panel are very likely to know the play so be certain of the context.

❑ **Can you interact?** . . . .

. . . .

. . . .

Shown through either the workshop (see page 110), or the interview (see workout 96).

Do you show potential?
If you are able to show all of the above, the chances are that you do show potential.

Remember: Nobody likes a know-it-all. Be open to learning and take heed of the suggestions of the audition panel should they make any.

Tip: If the panel choose to redirect your pieces, this can often be a sign that the audition is going well.

You need to be the best you can be in all of these categories if you are to stand a chance of progressing.

Audition requirements

Most theater schools will assess you on your ability to perform pieces of text. Often they will ask for two contrasting monologues: one from an earlier time period and one that is contemporary. In addition to this, you are likely to be required to take part in a group workshop and you may also have to do a short interview.

Choosing your audition speeches

Choosing pieces that suit you is essential. Here are some other important points to consider.

Read the requirements for each school carefully.
• Some schools specify exact speeches while others give you freedom of choice.
• Some schools require you to prepare one, two, or even three speeches and may even require you to sing.
• Some schools want speeches of 2 minutes while others require your pieces to be 3 or sometimes 4 minutes long.

> **Tip: Select pieces to showcase your skills**
> *Choosing a serio-comic piece instead of pure comedy gives you much more opportunity to show depth to your work (see workouts 81 and 82).*

Choose pieces that contrast

There is already a built-in contrast if one is classical and the other modern.

However, you should also consider the following:
• Make sure that one piece is dramatic and the other comic (or serio-comic).
• Contrast your staging. Try to ensure that one piece is very still while the other contains movement.
• Contrast your pacing. Choose one slow piece, the other more rapid.

> **Help!**
> I can't sing.
> • Choose a character song—in other words, a song that defines character and can be spoken and acted as well as sung (try "I Feel Pretty" from *West Side Story* or "I'm Getting Married in the Morning" from *My Fair Lady*). Have a couple of lessons with a singing teacher to perfect the timing.

> **Tip: Never over-run**
> *There is likely to be a time limit set for each of your monologues. This is usually 2 or 3 minutes. It varies from school to school. Never go over the required length of the monologue. Slightly shorter is much better.*

Use your natural accent or dialect

- Choose a modern piece that can be performed in your natural dialect.
- Even though classical pieces from earlier time periods may require the professional actor to speak in a classical accent or dialect, you do not have to do so. For example, if you are asked to perform a piece of Shakespeare you may do so using your own accent.

Choose pieces that fall within the range of your personality, age, and appearance. Play to your strengths. If you are a quiet, intense type of person who finds too much movement difficult, do not choose speeches that require you to be over-the-top or flamboyant. Characters can still be contrasting without being at opposite ends of the spectrum, so do not be tempted to play a character that is too much of a stretch for you just because it offers an obvious contrast.

Do not, under any circumstances, play a very old character unless you are very old. Likewise, do not play a young child. If you are around 18 years old, think of playing a character around 18–25. If you are in your early twenties, think 18–30. If you are 30 then your playing age is nearer 25–35. The age does not have to exactly correspond to yours, but it does have to be within the realms of believability.

Avoid characters that could be played by either sex, such as Puck from *A Mid-Summer Night's Dream* or Ariel from *The Tempest*. This is because it is hard to establish depth of character with these more androgynous beings. Also, never be tempted to play cross-gender characters, such as girls playing boys or vice versa—this type of characterization is too easily stereotyped.

Help!
Where do I find speeches?
- These can be chosen from plays you've seen. Maybe you're studying a play at school? However, most young actors getting ready for theater school choose their speeches from monologue books. There are many of these on the market. These contain around 50 monologues each. Choose one, read the play, and you're on your way; there are specific recommendations on pages 120–126.

Tip
Even if you are using your own accent or dialect, you still need to be true to the text. Whatever you do, do not change the words to suit you. You must be word perfect.

Help!
Can I use a speech from a movie?
- Most theater schools will say that you can. However, unless you are going to be auditioning on camera, avoid speeches from movies. Monologues designed for stage are closer to what you are doing (performing to a panel) and nearly always contain more opportunity for subtext.

Workout

83 Choosing a speech

Preparation
Look at some monologue books.

What to do
Isolate all the monologues that suit your age range and type. Choose the one that attracts you the most, i.e. one that you find personally sad or dramatic, or one that suits your sense of humor. Get the play. Study the

context. Study the character. Learn the speech.

Duration
As long as it takes to get it right. This is important. Repeat the process for as many speeches as you are likely to need.

Help!
What if all the monologues are too long?
- Most monologues will be longer than 2 or 3 minutes, so cut them at an appropriate place. This usually means at a natural pause in the text.

Staging your piece

"Staging" your monologue means figuring out where to stand and when to move. But before you can do this you need to know what is around you in the performance space. You need to construct your set. In an audition situation, most of your set will be in your imagination. Do not under any circumstances bring bits of furniture into the audition room—no matter how important you think they are to the piece. The only scenery you will be using will be chairs, and these are usually provided. Keep it minimal. The rest is up to your imagination.

If you have a choice of chairs, always choose the plainest ones; not those you think are closest to the style of the piece. You want to be showing off your acting against a blank canvas.

Exactly the same is true of your use of props (things you carry or use on stage such as an umbrella or a handbag). Use none at all, perhaps with the exception of a simple object such as a handkerchief. On the whole, it is very wise to choose pieces that do not require too much scenery or too many props. Costuming follows the same principles. For example, if your piece requires you to put your hands in your pockets then make sure that your trousers have pockets! However, you do not need to wear trousers that resemble that particular time period. Practice skirts are allowed (these are black wrap-around skirts used for character and classical work). However, they are by no means essential. In fact they are, more often than not, a hindrance. If you do decide to use one, then practice in it first.

Workout

84 Working out your set

Preparation
Pen and paper. A monologue of your own choice. An empty space.

What to do
Imagine the room in which the monologue is set. Write or draw the broader details such as the doors, windows, and furniture. Now go into much more detail—include colors and textures until you have recreated the entire environment. Now stand up and walk around your imaginary room, discovering whether or not the room is comfortable for your character, or perhaps even dangerous. Ground yourself in the imagined space and explore it all. As you are doing so, notice the imaginary details you have decided upon; you may even notice some more!

Duration
20 minutes writing.
20 minutes walking.

Workout

85 Miming 1 (props)

Preparation
Fill a briefcase or bag with five different items. For example: a pen, papers, a book, sandwiches, a wallet.

What to do
Open the bag and remove the objects one at a time. Make sure you make a mental note of where you place them. Return the objects to the bag. Close the bag. Repeat 3 or 4 times using exactly the same sequence and placing the objects in exactly the same places. Notice every little detail about your movements. Now repeat the whole thing in mime keeping your movements identical to when you were actually handling the objects.

Duration
Repeat 5 times alternating reality and mime.

What you want
For everything to be clear and seem unrehearsed.

What you don't want
To break the audience's sense of reality by not believing in you. This will happen if you put down an imaginary cup of coffee and pick it up from a different place. Even if you are only a fraction out, the audience will notice this and the believable environment you have created will be lost.

Tip
Always do this type of workout before you mime anything in a piece of drama. Also, return to the exercise regularly as it is easy to lose the detail in your work.

Workout

86 Miming 2 (details)

Preparation
A blanket or duvet.

What to do
Imagine that somebody has attached a tiny open pin to your blanket. You are tired, irritated, and all you want to do is go to bed. However, the pin may scratch you if you do. Carefully search the whole blanket to find it.

Duration
If this exercise is done correctly it should take 10–15 minutes. Remember that even though you are tired and irritable you must search meticulously. Commit totally to the exercise.

What you want
To use a small circle of attention (see workouts 58–62), so your search is natural.

What you don't want
To be thinking about the emotion you should be showing. Focus totally on the search and the rest will follow. Keep a sense of urgency to the search and keep true to the movement.

Acting with imaginary characters

You may need to imagine other characters from the scene being on the stage at the same time as you. You need to place them very carefully and know whether they are sitting or standing in order to place your eye line accurately when you are talking to them. Often, inexperienced actors place their eye lines too low; if the character they are talking to is seated, they tend to look to the back of the chair rather than a meter higher where the character's face is more likely to be.

Be careful not to upstage yourself. In other words, do not turn your back on the audience as you deliver your lines. If you place your imaginary characters behind you, the audience will see the back of your head when you turn to speak to them. It is also a mistake to place your characters directly to the side of you. At times like these, all the audience will see is your profile and therefore you lose the power of your performance.

If you are talking to one character, simply place the character either Down Stage Center Right (DSCR) or DSCL to the left of you. If you are talking to more than

Establishing eyeline.

Workout

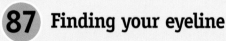

(87) Finding your eyeline

Preparation
Study monologue 7 (below).

What to do
Mother, Father, and Gerry are imaginary actors that you will interact with in this monologue. Imagine that when Gerry comes into the room he stands by the door and doesn't move throughout the piece. Remember that Mother and Father are sitting in the room. Establish eyelines with every character.

Practice the piece with someone standing in for Gerry so that you can gauge your eyeline. Pay special attention to keeping it constant while you sit, stand, and turn away (and then back again). Now practice without your stand-in there.

Duration
Repeat six times alternating between someone standing in for Gerry and someone not.

Monologue 7

He's gone too far this time. He really has. And Father, I know what you're thinking. I can tell from your face, but this has got to stop. I will have my say whether you like it or not.
[Enter Gerry]
There you are. I've got something to tell you. You're not going to like it but nevertheless it has to be said. I'm leaving Grangeworth Manor for good.
[Mother stands to leave]
Mother don't.

one character, spread them out in groups across the front on the stage.

Also remember to really "see" the character (or characters) you are talking to on stage. Make sure that you research their character(s) and your character's relationship to them. Make sure also that you know which lines they have just said to you—it is what they say to you that will prompt you to speak. To convince yourself that you are actually speaking to someone else, try to internalize the other character so that they are actually present to you.

If there are no other characters on the stage, and if your piece is seated and still, then for comic monologues place the chair center stage facing the audience. Be careful not to deliver the whole piece toward the panel; rather, treat them as part of an imagined, slightly larger audience. However, for dramatic monologues place the chair either center right or center left facing forward and slightly inward. Here your sight line is slightly past the panel but they can still see your face very clearly.

Practice your eyeline both standing and sitting.

Make the imaginary person as real as possible.

Workout

88 Finding your eyeline 2

Preparation
Use the same character and monologue as workout 87.

What to do
Place your characters so that you're not upstaging yourself. Work through the piece slowly paying close attention to your eyeline as you address the other characters. Get someone to sit in for each of the characters to check that your eyeline is correct. Rehearse the piece without anyone sitting in.

Duration
Repeat without anyone sitting in until it feels comfortable. Then get someone to sit in front of you so you can check that your eyelines are correct.

Stillness and pauses in movement and speech

While staging your piece it is very important to consider the pacing. For example, how fast does your character walk from A to B? Does he or she start off slowly and build up speed or slow down as they reach their mark? If so, why? Always be careful to keep the pacing realistic, otherwise it might seem that you are moving for the sake of it rather than because of something your character has been motivated to do. So make sure you subtly vary the pace of movement and speech within each piece, still keeping it within the realms of believability. Make sure there is a noticeable difference in the pace of your contrasting monologues.

Monologues

The use of stillness and pauses is equally important. They give your character a chance to think and feel (and the audience a chance to do the same). Here are three types of pause that can be used on any piece of text.

Emotional pause

Here, the words may stop or you may hesitate because the character is so overcome with emotion. Use this sparingly—or probably not at all unless you are indicated to in the text.

Sense pause

This is pausing at the punctuation marks. With modern pieces don't be too held by this type of pause. Make sure you find at least one or two moments in your monologue when you can go over a full stop or a comma without actually stopping. This will reflect natural speech and therefore make the pacing seem more realistic. It is also unnecessary to stop at every comma.

In fact, with modern pieces you can even stop mid-line when there is no punctuation at all. When performing, think of the punctuation more as a guideline than an imperative. In classical pieces, however, the punctuation must be much more rigidly observed.

Emphatic pause

This is a pause before or after a word or phrase to give it emphasis. For example: "I didn't hate him; I ...(pause) loathed him." Here the word "loathed" is emphasized so that the audience has more of an opportunity to feel the character's anger.

Reasons and actions

Your character does everything for a reason. For example, if you hold a telephone away from your ear it may be because the person on the other end is shouting. However, it could also be that you can't bear the person and don't want to hear what they have to say—or perhaps you are thinking about something else altogether. Remember that an action, whether it be closing a door or walking across the room, must be truthful and for it to be truthful your reasons for doing what you do must be crystal clear.

Workout Research

Preparation
Choose a monologue to use for your audition (or take one from pages 89 or 91 if you want to use this workout as an exercise).

What to do
Find out your character's motivations (the reasons for their actions). Ask yourself questions. Find out everything you can about the character.

Duration
As long as it takes to do some thorough research.

Tip
Always keep the staging simple in the audition. Although your pieces need to contrast (and so does your staging), there is no need to dash around. Remember that these are short pieces and therefore require less movement.

Workout Exploring movement in your monologue

Preparation
Select ten lines in your monologue where your character moves two or three times. This can be a movement such as turning the head, crossing the legs, leaning forward, or standing up. It can also be a larger movement such as walking across the room.

What to do
In line with your character's motivation, decide when in the script you are going to move and what that movement is going to be. Practice the entire section moving at a very steady and even pace, not using any pauses. Now rehearse the section again, this time varying the pace and adding appropriate pauses.

Duration
Repeat until you can make the varied pace seem realistic.

Tip
There may be large sections of your monologue in performance in which your character doesn't need to move at all.

Workout Exploring pacing and timing in your monologue

Preparation
Use the same monologue as workout 90.

What to do
Working with the same ten lines, decide in advance which words or phrases are the most important and where you are going to play your pauses. Decide on which type of pause you are going to use. Rehearse, keeping the pauses exaggerated and in the same places every time.

Duration
Keep repeating, gradually shortening the extended pauses until they seem natural. Repeat.

Tip
A pause in the text is also a great time to move.

 What you want
To keep it seeming spontaneous and natural.

What you don't want
To rush through your piece with everything occurring at the same pace.

Greek theater

Greek theater is the origin of all Western theater and was almost entirely based in Athens and its immediate surroundings. Athenian playwrights such as Euripides, Sophocles, and Aristophanes would write for the city Dionysia, a festival in honor of Dionysus, the god of wine and ecstasy. The plays would compete against each other with prizes and, above all, honor at stake. All the plays surviving from ancient Greece were written within less than a hundred years of each other, from 472–388 B.C.

The theater of Dionysus was where these competitions took place, in March or April of each year. The theater held 14,000 spectators at one time, in a huge semicircle around the stage (at that time it was called the "orchestra"). They sat on hollow, stone seats built into the hillside. This produced a natural raking system so that everyone could see. It also produced wonderful acoustics and the talented actor could be heard as clearly at the back of the auditorium as at the front. Some ancient theaters have survived intact but these were built somewhat later than the theater of Dionysus, and are nowhere near as big.

All of the actors wore masks and the actor would treat the mask with respect, as if it contained the soul of the character it portrayed. The number of actors was small and they would play various parts each, expertly changing mask, voice, and movement to suit. Supporting the actors was the Chorus. This contained 12 or 15 men and boys led by a lesser actor who also portrayed the Chorus' voice. The Chorus was incredibly important to the play as it gave it background pace, mood, and tone. The Chorus usually communicated in song form, commented on the play's themes, and generally represented the populace.

Playing Greek tragedy

Things to consider:

Characterization
The characters were larger-than-life and often embodied archetypes because the stories were nearly always drawn from ancient myth. For example, you may be playing a god, or, as in the case of Oedipus, a hero and king. Your character would be a "type" and what would have interested a Greek audience is the struggle your character underwent to conform to this "type."

Voice
Naturally, clarity of diction would have been extremely important because of the size of the arena and the fact that the actors were speaking from behind a mask. Also, vocal tone would have to be incredibly flexible and capable of a vast range to portray the wide variety of characters and their individual expressions.

Pacing
The pace of the speech and movement is precise. Every move is worked out beforehand with a view to creating the most dramatic effect possible. There would also be pauses for the chorus to react and respond to the other characters.

Workout

92 Playing Greek theater 1

Preparation
Study monologue 8 (below).

What to do
Rehearse the workout considering the following points:
• Stand tall and powerful, as if you are in a huge Greek theater. Begin to imagine filling a large space.

• For the purposes of the audition do not act as if you are wearing a mask.
• Remember to proclaim slowly and clearly.

Duration
Repeat until it becomes effortless.

Workout

93 Playing Greek theater 2

Preparation
Learn the section of monologue. Now consider your gestures—probably only two or three.

What to do
Perform the monologue considering all the points made in workout 92 adding gestures that would fill the space. Make sure that they are few and meaningful. Remember that you are communicating in a very large space.

Duration
Repeat until the "larger-than-life" style feels easy to you.

Tips: Study the text
• In Greek theater, always use the written punctuation (**1**).
• Pause after the word "father" for emotional effect (**2**).
• Pause after the word "mother," again for effect (**3**). Contrast the tones between "mother" and "father" to show how much you loved each of them.
• Pause briefly after "I" (**4**) to let the audience know what you think of yourself.
• Elongate the word "held," (**5**) imagining that you were being held: this line has a more violent feel so use a harder, more forceful tone of voice (**6**).
• Use a hard, short, sharp tone on "struck" to imitate the sound (**7**).

Monologue 8

Here is a quotation from "Oedipus the King" by Sophocles:
Oedipus: Polybus, [1] King of Corinth was my father [2]. A Dorian, Merope, was my mother [3]. And I [4] was held [5] in the realm of princes among the people there, [6] till I was struck [7] from out of nowhere...

Tip: Don't choose "Chorus"
Do not choose the part of "Chorus" as your audition speech as there is little opportunity to characterize and there are many particular and complicating factors to be considered.

Shakespearean theater

William Shakespeare was born in 1564 and died in 1616. During that time he wrote 38 plays. These plays fall into three distinct categories: comedies, tragedies, and histories. The comedies, such as *A Midsummer Night's Dream*, can be recognized because they often have extremely complex plots and recurring themes such as mistaken identity. The storyline will always end in marriage. The tragedies, such as *Hamlet*, have a more dramatic, violent tone and they always end in death. History plays, like *Henry V*, recount actual (and then dramatized) historical events.

Shakespeare's actors, who were all male, had to be very adaptable. Not only did they have to play a variety of parts, they had to be able to perform in many different locations. These ranged from gardens and palace ballrooms to theaters. Probably the most famous theater of the time was "The Globe" in London, which was opened in 1599 (and burned down in 1613). Good actors were hard to find and Shakespeare often wrote his major roles for specific actors.

There was no scenery on an Elizabethan stage. Even the theater offered only a pillar and a balcony. One of the techniques used to counteract this was called "quartering." Here the stage was divided into four, each section representing a different location in the play. The actors would simply move to the correct quarter and play the scene. During important monologues this would be abandoned and the actor would take center stage.

Shakespeare's audiences ranged from peasants to kings and queens (sometimes in the same theater at the same time), and his style of writing had to keep all levels of society entertained. The comedies would contain both slapstick, and a witty use of language. In the tragedies, bloody fighting, jealousy, and revenge contrasted with powerfully constructed imagery.

Performing Shakespeare today

Your audition panel will not be expecting you to perform your piece as if they were an Elizabethan audience. You need to show an understanding of the style but make it relevant to theater today. All of the work you've done so far still applies. You just need to add another level on top. Here are some basic guidelines:

- Make sure that you understand exactly what you are talking about and that you know the context thoroughly.
- Speak slowly and clearly.
- In rehearsal, allow the language to find its natural rhythm. This will happen if you respect the basic rhythm of the speech and follow the punctuation.
- Vary the length of the punctuated pauses considerably. For example, a period may be one second or five seconds in length. Remember to act (or move) through the pauses. As a general rule, don't pause in a speech for too long as it is easy to lose impetus and seem self-indulgent. Use the performance area as you would for a modern piece.

Use precise gestures when acting a Shakespearean piece. These must arise naturally from your emotion and not seem artificial. Remember that the emotion is still extremely real to your character. It is the body language that is more classically held.

Monologue 9

Male: Iago from the play "Othello" (Act 3, Scene 3, lines 391–395). Iago is expecting his general Othello (who is an African prince and army general) to promote him. When this does not happen Iago sets about to undermine and destroy him. He does this by leading him to believe that his wife is having an affair. Othello asks Iago for unmistakable proof in the short monologue below.

I see sir, you are eaten up with passion. I do repent me that I put it to you. You would be satisfied? But how my lord? Would you, the supervisor, grossly gape on?
Behold her topped?

✱ Key to Shakespeare's text
"Passion" means "anger and jealousy."
Line 2 means:
"I am sorry to be the one to tell you this news."
"Satisfied" means "have proof."
Lines 4 and 5 mean:
" Surely you don't want to watch them making love."

Monologue 10

Female: Portia from "The Merchant of Venice" (Act 3, Scene 2, lines 1–3). Portia, the heiress of Belmont, is in love with Bassanio. In order for her to marry him her father has set up a bizarre test in which Bassanio has to choose the correct box from three. Portia encourages him to wait awhile as guessing incorrectly means they must part forever.

I pray you, tarry. Pause a day or two Before you hazard; for in choosing wrong, I lose your company. Therefore forbear a while.

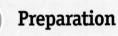

✱ Key to Shakespeare's text
"I pray you" means "I beg of you."
"Tarry" means "to wait."
"Hazard" means "to make a guess."
"Forbear" means "to withdraw."

Study these extracts. These are not full monologues but small acting studies, and are not long enough for an audition.

Workout

94 Playing Shakespeare

Preparation
Study the language of the extracts above. Make sure you know the meaning of what you're saying throughout your extract.

What to do
Read the appropriate extract aloud paying great detail to the punctuation. Now, still keeping the punctuation correct, experiment with the general pacing and timing, keeping the piece as natural as possible. Feel the forward movement of the text and pay attention to the naturally stressed or unstressed syllables and words.

Allow the emotion to be free so that the inflections occur naturally.

Duration
Repeat 10 times.

Tip: Don't ham it up
Just because you are performing a bit of Shakespeare, don't be tempted to put on an affected voice or a particular accent. Keep it clear and naturally placed.

Workout

95 Preparation

Learn the appropriate extract.

What to do
Stage the piece by adding a walk toward or away from your imaginary character. Add one or two gestures.

Duration
Keep running the piece through and experimenting until it feels comfortable.

Tip
If there is no punctuation at the end of a line you move straight onto the next without pausing.

The audition workshop

Most drama schools will ask you to take part in a practical workshop. This can take a number of different forms, ranging from a "group warm-up" or an "icebreaker" to a two-hour improvisation, movement, or even dance class.

Whatever you have to do, and however long it lasts, you need to remember that you are being watched—and this means you are being compared to the other people in the room. Stay focused on what you are being asked to do and don't let yourself be distracted by how others interpret the directions that you are all given. Have faith in your own instincts and don't try and second-guess how the auditioners are responding to you. Some schools may say that the workshop is not part of your assessment. Although they may think they are telling the truth, this is absolutely not the case. When you are watching something in this situation, you can't help but judge and compare. Remember, even if the panel are not observing, the person running the workshop is!

What they are looking for:
- Someone with natural vitality or "spark".
- Someone who is open and enjoys the work.
- Someone who is emotionally responsive.
- Someone who enjoys taking a risk.
- Someone who has a sense of honesty about their own work.
- Someone who is a team player.
- Someone who, during the exercises, works with focus, commitment, and humor.
- Someone who is grounded.
- Someone who knows what they think but is open to learning, and is not judgmental of others.
- Someone who they want to teach for three years.
- Someone who will be successful with training.

Here are some don'ts regarding the workshop:
- Don't go over the top. Energy and enthusiasm need to be natural, free-flowing, and very much a part of who you are.
- Don't take risks for the sake of it. (Taking a risk can just mean being free with your movement or being a little experimental with your ideas. Sometimes the simplest ideas are the best.)
- Don't feel that you have to cry your eyes out at the first possible opportunity. Play your characters with truth, depth, and sincerity.
- Don't criticize unless you are asked to. Remember "criticism" in its truest sense also means stating what was right as well as wrong. Make sure you give a positive point before the negative. Also, give the criticism as if you are genuinely trying to help the person rather than judging them. In other words: show you are aware of other people's feelings.
- Don't be a know-it-all. Don't disrupt the flow of the workshop by asking banal questions that you think make you seem clever. If you don't understand what to do, wait for a pause and confidently ask for an explanation. However, always feel free to engage in conversation with the workshop leader about the project, should the opportunity arise. If you are working with focus and commitment this says more than any conversation possibly could.

The interview

At some point during your audition you will be talked to on a one-to-one basis. This may be a scheduled interview, or perhaps during your monologue session. Here the main aim for the panel isn't only to test your knowledge, or indeed the content of your answers; it's more to see your natural personality. Remember to stay open and positive. Here is a question and sample answer:

Help!
What if I'm asked a question I don't understand?
• Don't panic. Just ask for clarification. If you still don't understand, then simply say something like: "I'm sorry. I don't know the answer to that one."

Tell me about a play you've enjoyed?

I really enjoyed *Equus* at the Phoenix Theater. Not only was I drawn into the incredibly complex emotional plot, but I was so moved (and surprised) by the performance of Daniel Radcliffe that I could hardly move from my seat. If he was aiming to convince people that he could play characters other than Harry Potter he certainly succeeded.

I must admit to being a closet Radcliffe fan but this was something else. It was such an open, brave, and raw interpretation for someone who is the same age as me. Perhaps that's why I empathized so much. He really held the stage and his timing was, well, brilliant, especially in the dramatic scenes. The silences really spoke and I believed every moment. I can't stop thinking about it even now. I can't wait to do that sort of thing myself. It makes me more determined to act than ever.

Here are some topics you may be asked to discuss:
• Tell me about a play you've enjoyed.
• What was the last play you saw?
• Why do you want to act?
• Why do you want to study at this particular drama school?
• Who do you admire in the world of acting?
• Who coached you in your drama pieces?
• Tell me about acting you've done outside of school.
• What can you tell me about your monologues (context, period, the playwright, etc.)?
• How did you enjoy the workshop?
• What's your first impression of the school?

Answering the questions
On the surface, the type of question you may be asked seems simple. However, don't be fooled into giving a simple answer. Begin by answering directly, then demonstrate your knowledge.

Workout

96 Practice interview

Preparation
Study the interview questions at left.
• Add some more of your own regarding the context of your monologue.
• Get someone to add some more of their own that have nothing to do with acting.

What to do
Get someone to ask you the questions in a type of mock interview.

Practice your answers.

Duration
Until you are happy with your responses.

Dos and don'ts

What you wear on the day reveals the type of person you are. First impressions in a situation like this really count. Here is a guide to costume, hair, and makeup for the big day.

Women

- Hair should be off the face. You should not need to be brushing it with your hand. Pin back long fringes. Have nothing elaborate in your hair. Keep it simple.
- Wear a very light, natural makeup.
- Do not wear perfume or any type of perfumed product.
- No jewelry that sparkles, protrudes, or catches the light. No large earrings (no large jewelry at all).
- Don't dress provocatively. You want people to look at your acting, not your chest.
- Choose colors you know suit you: certain colors, when worn close to the face, will make you look more radiant. Go to a clothing store and do some research on yourself. Avoid too much black.
- Wear pants that not only look good, but allow you to move freely.
- Don't wear clothes that have distracting logos or patterns on them.
- Wear comfortable shoes.

Be natural.

Don't dress like you are going out to a nightclub.

Workout

97 What to wear for the audition 1

Preparation
Using clothes from your wardrobe, dress as inappropriately as you possibly can for your audition. Try to make at least 10 mistakes.

What to do
Now look in the mirror and carefully assess each of the mistakes you've made.

Duration
30 minutes.

Men

- Hats and headwear will create shadows on your face. Avoid them.
- Messy hair is fine. Make sure that it is clean and does not cover your face. If it does, clip it back.
- Wear little or no makeup.
- No large jewelry—nothing that could hurt someone else when working spontaneously in your audition.
- Wear non-scented deodorant, even if you don't think you need it.
- Jackets are fine but remove them to act (unless they are needed for a character).
- Do wear a top that can be identified in a crowd. Nothing too obvious or garish.
- Research your colors and wear a top that suits your complexion.
- Make sure that your clothing is secure. For example, if you have to constantly pull your pants up, you won't be able to concentrate on your acting.
- Wear pants you can easily move in. Try to avoid sweatpants. They can look a little too casual for a formal audition.
- Wear sensible shoes.

The audition panel can see that you can play other characters.

The audition panel only sees someone hiding behind a look.

Workout

 What to wear for the audition 2

Preparation
Using clothes from your wardrobe, dress appropriately for your audition.

What to do
Study yourself in the mirror, checking your plus points. Ask people's opinions. Make a list of suitable clothes from your wardrobe. Make a list of items you may need to buy.

Duration
1 hour. (Really take your time to consider the best options.)

Tip
It is always worth bringing a pair of sweatpants and a T–shirt. Change into them if you find you have to do a very physical workshop before your monologues.

Tip
Practice your monologues in your audition clothes.

Help!
Do I need to change clothes between my audition pieces?
- No. This is not about costume; it is about acting. However, it's fine to slip on a jacket or practice skirt. If women choose to change from sneakers to heels between monologues, they should stick to black, and avoid anything that's too fancy.

48 hours before

Before the audition you will have to decide on the introduction to your monologues. It is imperative that you prepare it and that you don't leave it to chance on the day. The trick is to keep them short—very short. Also don't forget that you are not just "doing an introduction" but you are actually telling the panel which pieces you are going to perform, so make sure you communicate clearly with the people auditioning you. Balance the tone somewhere between formal and informal, keeping it natural and light. The introductions to your pieces (together with the interview) are the only times you address the panel directly, so make sure that you use plenty of natural eye contact.

Here is an example:
"My first piece is from *Much Ado About Nothing* by William Shakespeare, Act 2, Scene 1. I'll be playing Benedick." On the surface this may seem too concise. It is always tempting to put in facts such as who you are talking to, the plot, context, and mood of the piece. However, this is all unnecessary as you will be providing this information in your performance.

Tip
Very occasionally the panel may ask for more during your introduction. So be prepared to talk briefly about the context of the scene.

Tip
Wait until the panel is looking at you before you introduce your piece.

Workout

99 Preparing the introductions to your monologues

Preparation
Pen and paper.

What to do
Write the worst possible introduction to your pieces, and then the best.

Duration
Repeat the good introductions until you have memorized them. Practice them, along with your monologues, in front of a friend.

Tip: Hang on to your script
Do not give copies of your monologues to the audition panel unless you are specifically requested to do so. Leave them firmly in your bag or give them to a prompter if it is requested.

Preparing your piece 48 hours before

With 48 hours to go do not practice your pieces too much. As an exercise, run the words so that you're confident that you know them. It is advisable that before this time you will have had a couple of sessions with an acting coach. Some schools require that you have prepared with a coach. Even if they don't, it's a good idea to get some one-on-one expertise. Try to find a coach with a good track record of getting people into theater school. It is a helpful idea to have your final coaching session 48 hours before the audition. This will give you time to assimilate any new information given to you. Make sure you tell your coach that the audition is close as their approach might be different to a usual lesson. With 24 hours to go, work in the style of workout 48. Run your pieces through once in the morning and once in the afternoon. This will really get your mouth moving.

What you need to take with you

Make sure that you prepare everything you need to take. Here is a basic list:
Pen, paper, forms, accompanying paperwork, and identification. If you are asked to do a dance workshop, take a change of clothes. You might also take a change of shoes (only if necessary), some money, snacks, deodorant, and copies of your monologues.

Your workout program

With 48 hours to go, take your program down to half. The same applies to your physical program. With 24 hours to go, decrease them to just under a quarter.

Remember to run through a relevant selection of the previous exercises to get yourself ready. Review the tongue twisters to get your breath, voice, and tongue working together (workouts 42–51).

The day

Before you go to your audition do some voice exercises (see workouts 48 and 49). Run through each monologue once, just for words, and do some roll ups (see workout 8).

Dealing with nerves

Nerves are a positive thing. They are an intense reservoir of energy. They can help you do your best. However, if nerves always get the better of you, here's how to go about combating them on the day:

- Take control of your breathing. As you do, imagine that you are breathing in the atmosphere of the place and allowing it to settle inside you.
- Get involved in conversations with other actors who are auditioning. Don't be afraid to talk about nerves—it helps.
- Enjoy yourself. You have worked hard for this so give yourself a pre-audition pat on the back for getting this far.
- Don't be tempted to rush, especially at the beginning of things. If you're still incredibly nervous at the start of the monologue, take a moment to find the character's body language before you begin. Concentrate only on the first action you are going to perform.
- Be prepared for things to be different.
- Remind yourself before you go in that this will be a challenging environment in which to perform. Don't be taken by surprise.
- Look to technique for support.

If you are still so nervous that you can't think, focus on this absolutely basic technique: know that your serious piece, whether it be classical or modern, is all about being truthful. Know that your comic piece is all about exaggerated truthfulness.

Performing the monologues
(see pages 60–61)

Before you go into the room remind yourself of the introduction and the first two lines of the first piece. Unless you are very nervous, don't think about technique, but just allow yourself to act as you know you can. Remind yourself that this is what all the hard work's been about. You've practiced, so your technique should automatically support you.

Take your time. Do not, under any circumstances, rush into the room and shake the panel's hands enthusiastically. Simply walk in, smile, say hello, and wait, standing about 10 feet in front of the people you're going to be auditioning to. They are then likely to say something like: "So what are you going to do for us?" You answer this question, as a natural response, with your planned introduction. You then say something like: "May I use a chair" (if you need one) and you set your scene. Obviously each audition will be slightly different.

Once you have set your scene, take your opening position and pause for a moment or two in character. Then begin. Allow yourself to work with total commitment. Do not rush the work. At the end of the monologue, you hold the final position for a few seconds before letting the character go and returning to your natural posture.

Some schools, at this point, will redirect your piece. Be positive and professional. If you are unsure about a direction ask for clarification. Under no circumstances question the judgment of the changes you have been asked to make. Go with the flow as would a professional actor working with a professional director.

The workshop

Be relaxed with a professional attitude. Get involved, enjoy yourself, and enjoy working with other people. While working in a group engage in "active listening." This is the technique of really listening to what people (including the group leader) are saying. This gives them confidence. Make sure you then respond openly to what you have listened to. This is a great way of getting totally involved in the work.

If you are asked to watch other people perform, then watch with focus, and be open-minded and supportive. There may be other people auditioning with you who spend time talking about the amount of acting they've already done. Whatever you do, don't get pulled into this sort of competition. Don't boast about what you can do; show what you can do.

Workout

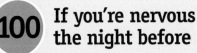

100 If you're nervous the night before

Preparation
Pen and paper.

What to do
Imagine the day. Write a list of all the things that could possibly go wrong. Now write a list of exactly how you would deal with them.

Duration
As long as it takes.
Be thorough. 1 hour.

What if I go wrong in the monologue?
Keep going. If you forget your lines simply pause, in character, and wait for them to arrive. If you go horribly wrong near to the beginning then you may ask to start again. However, this is not a good thing as most auditions run to a tight time frame. If it happens, move forward in a positive frame of mind. Prove to the panel by your work in the second piece that you can really act.

Program 6: week 6

This is your final program; the one you stick to and repeat until the auditions are over.

Morning Session (45 minutes)

Workout 1
Basic lying down.

What to do:
Lie down in the basic lying down position.
Duration:
5 minutes.
Aim:
Release the tension in the body. Add workout 50, page 55 for 10 minutes.

Workouts 4 and 5
Baby in a buggy/ Rolling baby.

What to do:
Baby in a buggy coming up into Rolling baby.
Duration:
Baby in a buggy for 3 minutes.
Rolling baby for 5 repetitions each way.
Aim:
Increase flexibility and strength.

Workouts 34 and 35
Adding sound to the breath.

Duration:
Do 10 repetitions of each workout. Take a short break in between but continue to lie down in the basic lying down position.
Aim:
Strengthen the breathing and connect the sound to the breath.

Workout 10
Preparation for neutral walking 2.

Duration:
Repeat the exercise 5 times. Then take a break before repeating again.
Aim:
Continues to strengthen basic posture.

Workouts 37 and 38
Resonating the voice.

Duration:
Repeat each workout on 5 breaths.
Aim:
Increase vocal resonance.

Weekly

Aim:
To practice contextualizing a character.

What to do:
Read at least one play per week. Choose a character. Research the time period and place. Look at what the text reveals about your character. Use your imagination to bring the character to life.

Everyday life

Workout 17
Walk in the park 1: go for a walk in the park twice a week to get the body used to neutral positioning.

Workout 39
Walk in the park 3: do this workout for 15 minutes, twice a week. This will strengthen your vocal resonance.

Workouts 23-26
Observational workouts: do one workout from 23–26 twice a week. These observational exercises will help you to become aware of tension in both yourself and others.

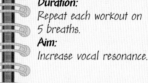

Evening Session (45 minutes)

Workout 3
Advanced lying down.

What to do:
Lie down in the basic lying down position.
Duration:
10 minutes (instead of 5) of lying down before starting the movement.
Aim:
Release the tension of the day before working on strengthening the back.

Workouts 5 and 6
Rolling baby/Baby trying to crawl.

Duration:
5 slow repetitions of Rolling baby coming into 3 minutes of Baby trying to crawl.
Aim:
Increase flexibility and strength.

Workout 8
Rolling down the wall.

What to do:
Gently roll up and down one vertebra at a time.
Duration:
3 slow repetitions.
Aim:
Balance and align the spine while standing.

Workout 33
Spontaneous breathing 2.

What to do:
Extinguish the three candles in sequence.
Duration:
Repeat 5 times. Rest in between.
Aim:
Strengthen the diaphragm.

Workout 43
Connecting the vowel sounds to the hum 2.

Duration:
Repeat 5 times as workout states.
Aim:
Connect the vowel sounds to the breath.

Workout 44
Connecting consonant sounds to vowel sounds.

What to do:
Run through the workout using the sounds specified.
Duration:
1 repetition.
Aim:
Strengthen the consonant sounds.

Workouts 48 and 49
Energizing the mouth.

What to do:
Repeat each tongue twister with your finger in your mouth, then repeat each tongue twister holding the tongue, then repeat each tongue twister through speaking normally.
Duration:
Repeat the above sequence twice.
Aim:
Energize and free the mouth.

Mini Program 6

Morning session (15 minutes)
Workout 1:
Lie down in the basic position for 5 minutes.

Workout 3:
Repeat this workout for 10 minutes.

Everyday life (15 minutes)
Workout 17:
Walk in the park 1. Once a week.

Workout 39:
Walk in the park 3. Walk in the park for 15 minutes. Twice a week.

Workouts 23-26:
Observational workouts. Choose one workout from 23-26. Twice a week.

Evening session (15 minutes)
Aim:
To practice contextualizing a character.

What to do:
Read at least one play per week. Choose a character. Research the time period and place. Look at what the text reveals about your character. Use your imagination to bring the character to life.

Monologues

Choose a monlogue that suits you. Make sure that the age range is correct and that the accent in which you are speaking is as close as possible to your natural accent and dialect. Below are some contemporary and classical monologues for you to explore. It may be that one of the prescribed monologues suits you perfectly. If not, have a look through the suggested monologue collections on page 126 to find your perfect piece.

CONTEMPORARY • FEMALE MONOLOGUES

The Marriage
• Nikolai Gogol (1842)

Act 1 Scene 3

Character: **Agafya**
First line: "I'm in quite a quandary. If only there were but one gentleman… " (May vary slightly due to different translations)
Last line: "I'll be a good girl: let fate decide."
Publisher: **Methuen World Classics**
Context: **The play is set in St Petersburg, Russia, 1830. It tells the story of a young lady who lives with her aunt and is still not married. Her aunt hires a matchmaker to bring suitors to the house for her niece to meet. Agafya thinks all four young men have their own special qualities and when pressed to make a choice, she just can't decide.**

In the speech we see Agafya agonizing over which man to marry. She finds a device to make her choice easier, which is to write all the mens' names on a piece of paper and pick one blindly and at random.

You must understand the social context of this play before you can approach this character and speech. The period of the play will inform your choices, and therefore inhibits anything too contemporary. Remember that the stakes are high for Agafya to make the right decision. Find images for each of the gentlemen you talk about.

Look Back In Anger
• John Osborne (1956)

Act 3 Scene 2

Character: **Alison**
First line: "It doesn't matter! I was wrong, I was wrong!"
Last line: " Don't you see! I'm in the mud at last! I'm groveling! I'm crawling! Oh, God—"
Publisher: **Penguin**
Context: **The play is about a love triangle between an intelligent, angry young man (Jimmy Porter), his upper-middle class, emotionless wife (Alison), and her stuck-up best friend (Helena). Cliff, the sociable Welsh lodger, attempts to keep the peace.**

Alison's speech is highly charged and emotional and comes at the end of the play, after having lived through their very volatile and abusive relationship. She is now broken and is confessing that she has lost their unborn baby, and is willing to forgive Jimmy.

This is a very cathartic speech and must be kept vulnerable and simple, avoiding anything sentimental.

The Good Doctor
• Neil Simon (1973)

Act 1 Scene 6

Character: **Wife**
First line: "No! … Not a word! … Not a sound!"
Last line: "I wish life brings you the happiness you have just brought to me."
Publisher: **Samuel French**
Context: *The Good Doctor* **is set in Russia during the 19th century and is loosely based on Anton Chekhov's comic short stories. It's a sequence of scenes that each tell a story.**

In the story of "The Seduction," the righteous and happily-married wife is being pursued by Peter Semyonych, a notorious womaniser and good friend of her husband. She is determined not to succumb to his good looks and charm, but in the end cannot resist his persistent courtships, and falls head over heels in love with him.

The speech is a straightforward and heartfelt confession of her undying love for him.

Find how you can relate to this character. Get an image of the kind of woman you are. Who is Peter? Can you imagine he's someone in your own life? Or do you have to draw from your imagination? Find a focus for where he might be standing—don't use anyone on the audition panel.

Work out your objective and break down your text to transitive verbs (see page 121, top right corner).

Actioning your texts

Try breaking down the text into transitive verbs. A transitive verb is an action verb. You have to pinpoint all the active verbs in your monologue—for example, to beg, to entice, to charm.

The actor should find the right verbs to fit the action of the monologue. The verb can change as many times as you change your thought/action. This is called "actioning" your text.

Between Daylight And Boonville
• Matt Williams (1983)

Act 1

Character: **Marlene**
First line: **"This one time, before the kids were born... "**
Last line: **"Don't ever go to bed angry."**
Publisher: **Samuel French**
Context: **The play is set in a temporary trailer camp in the strip-mining country of Southern Indiana.**

In the play we see three miners' wives and their kids while away the time in the "recreation area" of their trailers as their husbands are away working. We learn of their dissatisfaction with their lives. Marlene's best friend Carla is packing to run away, and Marlene, who is almost seven months pregnant, tries to convince her she doesn't have the perfect marriage that Carla believes she has.

In this speech, Marlene recounts a story of a big fight she had with her husband before the kids were born, but makes the point that ending the fight well is the secret to an enduring marriage.

Since the play is set in the South, you must have at least the essence of a Southern accent. Work out your motivation and break the text down accordingly into transitive verbs. The most important thing to remember is to get the images for what you're saying and to live it—make it real, like it really happened.

Blue Window
• Craig Lucas (1984)

Act 1 Scene 3

Character: **Libby**
First line: **"(It was a) Big Wedding. And... we laughed. Marty... "**
Last line: **"I can't have anybody hold me. I can never be held."**
Publisher: **Samuel French**
Context: **The play is set simultaneously in five separate, contemporary apartments in NYC.**

Scene 1 is a series of complex overlapping scenes. We see Libby preparing for a dinner party with a group of friends who don't know each other. She is horrified when the cap on one of her teeth falls out. Scene 2 is the dinner party. Scene 3 follows one of the guests, Norbert, as he stays after the party and makes (unrequited)advances toward her.

In this speech we learn that she has been acting strange all evening due to a traumatic event that resulted in the tragic death of her ex-husband.

The speech is confessional—it's not easy for Libby to open up. We must see her inner struggle as she recounts this horrific and graphic event. Some of her story is reflective, so be careful not to sentimentalize it. You must be truthful and visualize the images in order to share this tale.

MALE MONOLOGUES

Ah, Wilderness!
• Eugene O'Neill (1933)

Act 4 Scene 2

Character: **Richard Miller**
First line: **"Must be nearly nine... "**
Last line: **"There she comes now."**
Publisher: **Samuel French**
Context: **The play takes place in the Miller's family home in Connecticut on the fourth of July in 1906. The play focuses on the adolescence and coming of age of Richard Miller, who dabbles in poetry, politics, falling in love, and heartbreak.**

In the speech we see Richard on the beach nervously awaiting his girlfriend, Muriel, whose father had forbidden to ever see him again after reading some of the love poetry he had written for her. Distraught, he spends a drunken night in a bar with a prostitute. In his drunken state he realizes how much he loves Muriel and is desperate to see her again. He arranges to meet her secretly at the beach, but is scared that she won't be able to escape from her father.

In order to play this truthfully, you must understand the period in which the play was written. The speech has to abound with natural lyricism, innocence, and naivety, otherwise the piece won't work.

CONTEMPORARY • MALE MONOLOGUES cont.

Tracers
• John DiFusco (1980)

Act 1, "Initiation"

Character: **Dinky Dau**
First line: **"I remember the sky was overcast."**
Last line: **"You're dead, motherfucker!"**
Publisher: **Dramatists Play Service**
Context: **The play is about the Vietnam war. It was written from first-hand experience by the actors who were there. It's graphic, gripping, and moving, using rock songs as a backdrop and stories to bring alive the harrowing accounts.**

The speech from Dinky Dau recounts an attack from the enemy in the middle of the fields. It is very descriptive and physical. It would be impossible to approach this speech without an understanding of the war in Vietnam. This speech is very visceral—you must physically embrace what you are describing and connect to what you are saying.

A Lie of the Mind
• Sam Shepard (1985)

Act 1 Scene 3

Character: **Jake**
First line: **"She was goin' to these goddamn rehearsals every day."** (Cut the dialogue in between to make it a monologue.)
Last line: **"And she was trying to convince me that I was crazy."**
Publisher: **Dramatists Play Service**
Context: **The play is set in the American West. The story flips between two desperate families that are linked through marriage. A savage incident of spousal abuse changes all their lives, until the distressing incident that occurs at the end of the play.**

Jake has just returned home after shooting his wife in the head, leaving her with potential brain damage. He tries to justify himself to his brother by explaining what led him to this wild act of jealousy.

However hard it might be to defend Jake's actions, that's exactly what you need to do in order to play the speech. You must be clear in your objective to convince your brother that you were driven to this by pure jealousy, caused by her actions. You must feel vindicated—you were right, and she got what she deserved.

Roberto Zucco
• Bernard-Marie Koltès (1988)

Scene 6, "Metro"

Character: **Roberto Zucco**
First line: **"I'm just a normal, sensible young man who never draws attention to himself."**
Last line: **"I'm like a hippopotamus moving very slowly through the mud, whose chosen path and pace nothing can alter."**
Publisher: **Methuen**
Context: **The play is based on a true story of an Italian serial killer who murdered several people in Europe. It follows Roberto Zucco on his dark adventure, committing sinister, dreadful crimes without motive.**

The speech takes place on a bench on a deserted train platform in France. Roberto is sitting next to an old man who's also missed the last train and they are both locked in until the station opens again in the morning. The old man, uneasy with the situation, asks Zucco to talk about himself. Zucco presents himself as a normal, likeable, guy.

The challenge of the piece is to find the external façade of an everyday kind of a guy, but underneath it all, reveal something evil, dark, and sinister. There's a lot of subtext in this speech. The inner nature of Zucco has to be very subtly bubbling beneath the surface.

SHAKESPEAREAN • FEMALE MONOLOGUES

Mojo
• Jez Butterworth (1995)

Act 2 Scene 2

Character: **Baby**
First line: **"I was about nine, bit younger."**
Last line: **"Then when we'd finished, we got back in the cab and drove back to town. Covered in blood."**
Publisher: **Nick Hern Books**
Context: **The play is a black comedy set in a sleazy Soho rock 'n' roll club in 1958. We watch as small-time hustlers try to break out of their low-life, petty criminal ways in order to get a big-time break, but without much success.**

The speech is an amusing story told to Silver Johnny, who's gagged and hanging upside down—there's something very enjoyable and liberating about telling a story to someone who can't answer back. You must get full mileage out of this by clearly painting the picture and capturing the humor behind it. Relish the descriptions and play it truthfully.

Henry VI Part 1
• William Shakespeare (c.1588)

Act 1 Scene 2

Character: **Joan la Pucelle**
First line: **"Dolphin, I am by birth a shepherd's daughter."**
Last line: **"If thou receive me for thy warlike mate."**
Context: **Takes place in France at the battlefield near Orléans. Joan of Arc turns up unexpectedly to talk to Charles the Dauphin about one of her visions. She wishes to help lead the opppressed French to victory in the seige of Orléans.**

Joan is an uncomplicated character. Her speech is straightforward and understated. She offers partnership in order to win the war.

When you approach this speech try to connect to how important the war is to Joan. Totally commit to your conviction.

Richard III
• William Shakespeare (c. 1591)

Act 1 scene 2

Character: **Lady Anne**
First line: **"What, do you tremble? Are you all afraid?"**
Last line: **"Which his, hell-governed arm hath butcher'd!"**
Context: **Takes place in London, in a street funeral procession. Richard of Gloucester blocks the way. Lady Anne is enraged by his meddling—he has already murdered her husband, the previous King.**

The speech is a torrent of abuse against Richard, and is visual and provocative.

You must embrace the language in particular—the vowel sounds carry the strong words of revenge.

SHAKESPEAREAN • FEMALE MONOLOGUES cont.

A Midsummer Night's Dream
• William Shakespeare (c.1595)

Act 1 Scene 1

Character: **Helena**
First line: **"How happy some o'er other some can be!"**
Last line: **"To have his sight thither and back again."**
Context: **Takes place in Athens in the palace of Theseus. Helena is in love with Demetrius, who's in love with Hermia, Helena's best friend. Hermia and her suitor Lysander are planning to run away to get married. Hermia tells Helena of her plans to elope, and hopes that her leaving will change Demetrius' affections for her.**

In this speech, Helena woefully expresses her confusion about love. She feels a lot of pain and is open about her feelings of jealousy and grief. She is negative about the situation in which she finds herself.

To play Helena, you must recognize her low self-image and childlike disposition, and try to relate to her situation.

Julius Caesar
• William Shakespeare (c.1599)

Act 2 scene 1

Character: **Portia**
First line: **"You've urgently, Brutus, stole from my bed."**
Last line: **"Dear my Lord, make me acquainted with your cause of grief."**
Context: **Takes place in Rome, in Brutus's garden, the night before he assassinates Julius Caesar.**

Here we see Portia trying to pacify her restless husband by emotionally pleading with him. Her language is strong and provoking.

In playing Portia you will have to find the frustration and anger she feels toward her husband.

The Winter's Tale
• William Shakespeare (c.1611)

Act 3 Scene 2

Character: **Hermione**
First line: **"Sir, spare your threats."**
Last line: **"Apollo be my judge."**
Context: **Takes place in Sicilia, in a court of justice. Hermione is noble, virtuous, and dignified. She's married to the King, Leontes, who wrongly accuses her of being unfaithful to him.**

Hermione has been brought to trial and is fighting to defend her innocence. She tries to vindicate herself by being eloquent, rational, and unemotional.

You must try to embody Hermione's dignity and understand how unjust it is to be accused of something that you just didn't do. Understand that you are fighting for your life.

MALE MONOLOGUES

Henry VI, Part 2
• William Shakespeare (c. 1590)

Act 5 Scene 2

Character: **Young Clifford**
First line: **"Shame and confusion."**
Last line: **"Nothing so heavy as these woes of mine."**
Context: **Takes place near St Albans on a battlefield. A major battle has just ensued with big losses. John Clifford, a young follower of King Henry, enters to discover the body of his dead father, Lord Clifford who was killed by Richard, Duke of York.**

In the speech, we see Clifford lament over his father's body. It's very emotional, and full of grief and anger over the effects of the war on humanity. He wants revenge on the Duke and the entire House of York.

There's a focus and journey in this speech—it starts with bewilderment and ends in resolution.

Much Ado About Nothing
• William Shakespeare (c.1598)

Act 2 Scene 1

Character: **Benedick**
First line: **"O, she misused me past the endurance of a block."**
Last line: **"I would to God some scholar would conjure her, for certainly... "**
Context: **Takes place in Messina, in Leonato's house. Benedick is being set up by Don Pedro. There's a plot to make Beatrice and Benedick fall in love. Beatrice has just made fun of him at a masked ball, and he feels humiliated by her.**

In the speech we see his overreaction to her insults. We should believe Benedick is very hurt by her words and can't contain his anger and embarrassment over her outrageous remarks. We should also feel that Benedick, although reacting so strongly, is also falling in love with Beatrice.

Henry V
• William Shakespeare (c.1599)

Act 3 Scene 2

Character: **Boy**
First line: **"As young as I am, I have observed these three swashers."**
Last line: **"Their villainy goes against my weak stomach, and therefore I must cast it up."**
Context: **Takes place in France at the battle of Harfleur. A boy servant talks to the audience in prose about wrong doing and weakness in times of war.**

Using uncomplicated language and humor, there is a very colloquial feel to this speech. The boy is wise in his observations about criminal and immoral activity. By the end, we see how vulnerable and sickly he has become due to the misdemeanors of war.

The approach to this speech must be simple and truthful.

SHAKESPEAREAN • MALE MONOLOGUES cont.

King Lear
• William Shakespeare (c. 1603)

Act 1 Scene 2

Character: **Edmond**
First line: **"Thou, Nature, art my goddess."**
Last line: **"Now gods, stand up for bastards!"**
Context: **Takes place in England at the Earl of Gloucester's castle. Edmond is the bastard son of Gloucester. This is his first appearance in the play. He enters reading a letter and we understand who he is through his speech.**

To play Edmond, you must *recognize* he's a villain, but not *play* a villain. You must completely justify your character's actions but not comment on them.

The speech is fast-paced. His feelings about his birthright and territory are made clear. He is fervent about his opposition to his brother Edgar.

King Lear
• William Shakespeare (c. 1603)

Act 2 Scene 3

Character: **Edgar**
First line: **"I heard myself proclaimed, and by the happy hollow of a tree escaped the hunt."**
Last line: **"Edgar I nothing am."**
Context: **Takes place in England at Gloucester's castle. Edgar is the legitimate son of Gloucester who is accused by his bastard brother, Edmond, of plotting to kill their father and take his land.**

Edgar talks to the audience and decides to disguise himself and run away. During the speech, he slowly transforms himself into "Poor Tom." He tries to talk like a mad beggar and knows it is imperative to be convincing in order to escape.

The actor has to be believable in this transformation, and recognize the high stakes of the situation.

MONOLOGUE COLLECTIONS

Audition Monologues for Student Actors
by Roger Ellis
(Meriwether Publishing)

Monologues for Actors of Color: Women
by Roberta Uno
(Routledge: A Theatre Arts Book)

Monologues for Actors of Color: Men
by Roberta Uno
(Routledge: A Theatre Arts Book)

The Actor's Book of Contemporary Stage Monologues
by Nina Shengold
(Penguin)

American Theatre Book of Monologues for Women
by Stephanie Coen
(Theatre Communications Group)

American Theatre Book of Monologues for Men
by Stephanie Coen
(Theatre Communications Group)

Monologues for Young Actors
by Lorraine Cohen
(Avon)

Contemporary American Monologues for Women
by Todd London
(Theatre Communications Group)

Contemporary American Monologues for Men
by Todd London
(Theatre Communications Group)

The Ultimate Scene and Monologue Sourcebook
by Ed Hooks
(Watson-Guptill: Back Stage Books)

Index

Credits

Thank you to Debbie Rowe for all photographs of the models. The publisher thanks the following for permission to use photos: p.10 Shutterstock; p.33 Shutterstock; p.35t Warnerbros/The Kobal Collection/Marshak, Bob; p35b Miramax/The Kobal Collection.

All other images are copyright of Quarto Publishing plc. Quarto apologizes for omitting any credits.

Monologues on pages 120–126, chosen and contextualized by Dee Cannon, the main acting teacher at the Royal Academy of Dramatic Art (RADA) in London, UK. A renowned international freelance acting coach and director working all over the world in television, film, and theater, visit her website at www.deecannon.com.

Models featured are Orlando Clarkson, Theo Garman, Camille Giraudeau, Francesca Hole, Loz Keystone, Boris Mitkov, Alex Roe-Brown, and Louise Williams.

Thank you to the Arts Educational School, London.